Wakefield Press

Mothers in ARMS

Meg Hale is a former social worker and government investigator who lost a child to adoption in South Australia in 1968. Working as ARMS's first social worker in the 1980s she helped South Australia pass the first laws in the English-speaking world giving mothers the right to apply for identifying information about their children. Meg continues her work as an activist, advocating for the rights of mothers in adoption.

Mothers *in* ARMS

Forced adoption – mothers find a voice

MEG HALE

Wakefield
Press

Wakefield Press
1 The Parade West
Kent Town
South Australia 5067
www.wakefieldpress.com.au

First published 2014

Edited by Julia Beaven, Wakefield Press
Text designed and typeset by Wakefield Press
Printed in Australia by Griffin Digital, Adelaide

National Library of Australia Cataloguing-in-Publication entry

Author:	Hale, Meg, author.
Title:	Mothers in ARMS : forced adoption – mothers find a voice / Meg Hale.
ISBN:	978 1 74305 312 6 (paperback).
Subjects:	Australian Relinquishing Mothers Society.
	Association Representing Mothers Separated from their Children by Adoption.
	Adoption – Australia.
	Adoption – Moral and ethical aspects – Australia.
	Mother and child – Australia.
Dewey Number:	362.7340994

To Valma Gay, who was afraid and spoke up anyway,

and

to Maureen Craig, whose energy lasted the distance.

Contents

Acronyms

AASW	Australian Association of Social Workers
AMA	Australian Medical Association
ARMS	Australian Relinquishing Mothers Society, later known as Association Representing Mothers Separated from their children by adoption
ATOM	Australian Teachers of Media
NCSMC	National Council for the Single Mother and her Child
PASS	Post Adoption Support Services
SPARK	Single Pregnancy and After Resource Centre
WIS	Women's Information Switchboard

Foreword

I have had the honour of knowing Meg for thirty-four years. We are good and close friends. Over the years we have laughed and cried, and shared our hopes and dreams – and our deepest secrets. We have raised our children, overcome relationship breakdowns, and struggled through career challenges. We have buried our parents and lost dear friends along the way. But our bond has meant more than just friendship. It has allowed me to be part of a journey, both personal and political, from sadness and despair to empowerment, realisation and truth.

We all dream about changing the world, and know the adage: 'It only takes one person to make a difference.' But before we can start to dream we may need to change ourselves; or as Gandhi said, 'Be the change you want to see in the world'. In *Mothers in ARMS* Meg writes about a very personal struggle that made a difference. It demanded courage and determination. It led her to join a group of women who had the resolve to bring about major change, not just for themselves but for the many thousands of other women who shared the injustice and stigma associated with forced adoption in Australia. When I first met Meg she described herself as a 'bad girl' who had had her child taken from her. She wanted to check that this would not harm our friendship. She told me how a decision she had no choice about making impacted on her every day of her life. She described the overwhelming loss and sadness, and how she felt alone, angry and betrayed. These feelings never went away. She could not reconcile it. Knowing this did not harm our friendship, it strengthened it.

No one is more qualified to speak on the impact of a life-changing event than the person who experienced it. The writing of this book is the result of a healing process that has taken many years, and the changes it highlights have been significant personally and politically and impacted on many. I am proud that I have been able to share it.

Mothers in ARMS has all the ingredients readers look for in a book. It is about love, loss, conspiracy, political intrigue, injustice and prejudice. It tells of a growing awareness and confidence to stand up and fight back, and the courage to do it. And it challenges long-held societal prejudices, revealing the bitter impact forced adoption has had on so many lives.

Philippa Aston, OAM, PSM

Prologue

1968

An antiseptic hand pushed hard against the girl's chin, twisting her head to one side and pinning it into the rubber pillow. No one spoke but everyone in the delivery room knew it was to stop the girl from looking at her baby when it was born.

With her face suffocating under the weight of the nurse's arm, the girl gave one last push and the baby was delivered. And as quickly as it arrived, the muffled cry of new life disappeared behind a closed door. Resigned, the new mother focused her eye on the clock on the wall and saw that her child had been born at half past two in the morning.

The hospital almoner's voice was harsh and clipped as she reminded the girl that she must sign the adoption papers as soon as she left hospital. There was no point asking the almoner again why she had to give up her baby. The answer never changed. 'You're not married,' she would say. 'If you really love your baby you'll do the right thing and let it be adopted by a married couple who will give it a life you would never be able to provide. It would be selfish of you to keep it.'

The girl touched the tiny wrinkled hand and instinctively the fingers curled around her own, clinging tightly in some primal reflex. She stared in awe. 'You've got long fingers like me,' she whispered. 'I must remember that.'

The girl's head whirred as another hand pushed a Consent to Adoption form in front of her. A stiff voice said, 'Sign here,' and it snapped when the girl asked if it were true that she had thirty days to revoke her consent.

‘It would be selfish of you to change your mind. The baby will be with its new parents and it would be cruel of you to take it away from people who already loved it, now wouldn’t it?’

The girl signed the paper and thought how ironic it was that it should be called a consent when she felt she had been forced into it from the beginning.

The girl left the grey government building and stopped when she reached the footpath. She thought about the tiny baby she had left behind and how cruel it was that she should have to give up her child simply because she was unmarried. And as she disappeared down the street and into the anonymity of the crowd she muttered under her breath, ‘One day somebody will do something about this. This is so wrong.’ And quietly she added, ‘When you’re grown up, please come and find me if you can.’

1

The First Voices

IT WAS A WEEK before Mother's Day 1982 and mothers sat among the attendees at the Third National Adoption Conference in Adelaide. The women squirmed in their seats as they heard about the 'adoption experience' from the adoptive parents' point of view and they sighed when social workers talked about the mechanics of finding parents for unwanted babies. Apart from a few comments in one of the workshops no one mentioned the mothers at all.

On the second day a small group met on the conference lawns and under an umbrella the women planned the beginning of the mothers' movement. Marie Meggitt and Jo Clancy were members of the National Council for the Single Mother and her Child (NCSMC), a political group that had grown out of Parents Without Partners and that had been fighting for some years for the rights of any mother who had borne an exnuptial child. Marie and Jo had both lost babies through adoption and they had come to the Adelaide conference to make sure that mothers' experiences were being heard. Rosemary Kiely was another at the lawn meeting, a member of the NCSMC who had attended the conference in her capacity as media officer with Victoria's major benevolent society, The Brotherhood of St Lawrence. The mothers wanted to know how they should go about getting publicity for their new group. Rosemary suggested finding a name was a priority. Ideally it should include the words *relinquishing mothers* as that was a commonly accepted name for women who gave up their babies for adoption and as acronyms were popular Rosemary thought ARMS might be a punchy title for the group. It was visual and symbolic – empty arms and open arms. The words *Australian* and *Society* were added to complete the ARMS acronym, and after the name was settled Jo was delegated the responsibility of writing a speech to be delivered on the final day of the conference.

With the blessing of the convenors Jo announced the formation of a national Australian Relinquishing Mothers Society at the closing session of the adoption conference. The audience sat spellbound as she said relinquishing mothers had 'endured a gulag of suffering' and told what it had been like for young girls to have their babies taken from them and adopted out. Attendees listened, shocked, as Jo explained how it had been drilled into new mothers that they would be selfish to keep their babies. They were unmarried with no financial means of support and their children would be destined to a life of poverty and the stigma of illegitimacy if they remained in their care.

She stared intently at the audience as she spoke of the pillows and blankets put in front of girls' faces on the delivery table so they could not see their babies at birth, and how they were yelled at when they pleaded to hold their newborns just once before they were taken away.

Jo emphasised that these women had not wanted to give up their children and that they had been forced into it by almoners and social workers, doctors, priests and their own families. Their babies had been taken under duress, without care or compassion, and these kinds of adoptions were still going on well into the 1970s. ARMS was necessary, Jo said, to give relinquishing mothers the voice that had been missing from adoption until now.

When the conference was over the mothers returned to their home states where they gave media interviews announcing the birth of the national ARMS movement. By the end of the year Victoria, New South Wales, Western Australia and Queensland had formed associations to provide mutual support.

South Australia was strangely quiet, and in spite of it being the place where mothers had first united as a single entity, an ARMS group did not eventuate in Adelaide in 1982. There was, however, a small band of women from Jigsaw – the first organisation in Australia to help adoptees search for their parents and vice versa – already meeting in private to talk about their loss. Their role would be pivotal over the next thirty years of the adoption movement.

Jigsaw member Lila had been a single mother and she knew all about the prejudice faced by women who were unmarried and pregnant. Fortunately she was able to keep her child but her circumstances took a strange turn when, because of a legal anomaly, she had to adopt her own son so that her new husband could adopt him. Hence, she became an adoptive parent of her own child and the original birth certificate was cancelled.

Lila and Jigsaw mothers Joylene and Brenda were asked if they would look at starting a group specifically for relinquishing mothers. It was obvious that, although their search needs were similar to those of the adopted people in Jigsaw, mothers had different issues as well. It was thought that, as well as remaining part of the main Jigsaw group, they might benefit from being able to meet separately so they could talk openly about their experiences of loss, guilt and anger. It was from this idea that the first small group for mothers was formed, and in the safety of a private room they talked about what had happened to them. Of course they also compared notes on the best ways to try and find their now adult children.

2

Mother's Day Phone-in

A YEAR AFTER Jo Clancy's 'gulag of suffering' speech at the South Australian adoption conference, two young women from Adelaide packed overnight bags and headed for Melbourne. Harrison Anderson, co-ordinator of the Single Pregnancy and After Resource Centre (SPARK), and Ann Sharley, a social work student employed at the centre, were delegated to attend a joint conference of the NCSMC and the newly formed ARMS groups.

At the conference the young women were horrified to hear ARMS mothers talk of losing their babies. They were determined to find out whether this was a rare experience or a more widespread phenomenon hidden from society and even women's activists like themselves. Harrison and Ann's work at SPARK – an agency that worked primarily with single mothers who had kept their children – had connected them with many women who had suffered the stigma of unwed pregnancy and remembered the unrelenting pressure to give up their babies to married couples. Many times the only difference between women who kept their babies and the mothers who lost them to adoption was the support they had when leaving hospital.

A conference speaker read out that a quarter of a million women had lost a child through adoption in Australia and the room fell silent. The figure was far greater than anyone had imagined, and if only a small number of those mothers had experienced what the ARMS groups were saying then something had gone terribly wrong with adoption. Harrison and Ann, along with the rest of the delegates, voted to make sure that appropriate support was provided to mothers who had lost children through adoption, and that each State and Territory would push for law changes about past and future adoptions as a matter of urgency.

Harri and Ann could not sleep on the train, and as the old Overland rattled its way back home to South Australia they talked frenetically about what they had heard. Despite their own experiences (and Harri, herself, had gone through a single pregnancy and all the prejudice and pressure associated with it) they had not had reason to question the mythology about why girls adopted out their children. At that time adoption was not talked about from the perspective of the mother and the NCSMC conference was unique in opening a door to a hidden experience. This outpouring of grief galvanised the two young women into action. They made a commitment to find out how many other women shared this history, and what had contributed to them giving up their newborn babies.

The two travellers were also curious about why South Australia had not started an ARMS group when the others were established after the 1982 Adoption Conference and wondered if there might not be a local need at all. But Ann was about to start her final year social work placement and she was looking for something she could sink her teeth into. They decided to organise a phone-in on the Friday of the Mother's Day weekend to see if there was anyone else who had the same issues as the women interstate.

When they returned to work the next week the women set about looking for a venue for the Mother's Day phone-in. Their own office only had one telephone line and although no one really expected many calls Harri and Ann decided it might be better to err on the side of caution. The Women's Information Switchboard (WIS), an education and support service for women that had been running since 1978, had several phone lines and it was just the place to research a women's issue like this one. WIS did not hesitate in making three telephone lines available just on the off chance more than one phone might be needed. It also offered the services of a volunteer.

Having finalised the venue, press releases were sent out to all the major media outlets to publicise the phone-in. The release described relinquishing mothers as women who were made to enter into a contract. This set in motion the pretence that somebody else was the baby's real parent. Provocatively, the headline read 'We are looking at what may be the biggest cover-up in this country's history'. That was bound to get a response from someone!

On the day of the phone-in Harri and Ann arrived at WIS early, nervous but also curious about what calls they might get – if any. Someone scribbled out a short list as a guideline for the interviews. The questions included:

How did you feel in yourself at the time of adoption? (e.g. couldn't cope, no money, thought it would be best for the child and me)

How have you felt in yourself since the adoption and now?

What attracted you to adoption? (e.g. financial security, 2 parents etc)

What do you think of adoption now?

Would you like information about your child; if so would you like identifying, contact/access.'

With the questionnaire complete the two women and their volunteer sat with pens and paper at the ready, waiting for the phone lines to open. What happened next floored them.

As soon as the clock struck 9 am the three telephones started ringing – simultaneously. And as the receiver was put down on one call another one came in. And then another, and another, and another.

Some women were crying or inconsolable. Others were angry about what had happened to them. Many were just amazed that someone was taking the time to listen to their story. No one had ever listened to them before. In fact, no one had ever encouraged them to speak about it at all. It had been their terrible secret. Again and again the mothers talked about guilt, shame, loss, unresolved grief, and lack of choice. The questionnaire was useful but it did not take long before Ann and Harri realised it needed some adaptation. The question asking women what had *attracted* them to adoption had received vehement replies. Mothers said they had never been 'attracted' to adoption; it had been forced upon them. The word was duly scratched off the form, and by day's end no one was in any doubt about what these mothers were saying in relation to the myth that they had voluntarily abandoned their babies.

Ann and Harri had only planned to hold the phone-in on one day but as the three shell-shocked researchers turned off the lights and closed the doors they could still hear phones ringing in the darkness behind them. As they stepped out of the building and onto the street they knew they would be coming back the next day, and probably the day after that. It would be Mother's Day on Sunday and based on the first day's experience that day was going to be the busiest one of all. And they would certainly need more volunteers.

For the remaining two days the calls came in as quickly as they had on the first day and each story was as potent as the one before.

> 'They wouldn't tell me if I had a boy or a girl. I still don't know. That was twenty years ago,' one woman cried.

> 'I was so drugged I don't even remember signing the consent form and I never got a copy of it. I think it might have been illegal.'

> 'I was only sixteen,' another mother said. 'I walked away without my baby and with nothing to show that I had ever had a child.'

Women talked about having their breasts bound to suppress the flow of milk. Others said they had been put into hospital wards with mothers who were nursing their newborns, and that they cried themselves to sleep listening to babies suckling in the beds next to them. One woman said that she had been in a church home where she had been made to breastfeed her baby for three months before giving it up. 'They wanted a nice chubby little baby,' she said. 'I don't think anyone cared about what it was doing to me.'

Most women said they had been told over and over again that it would be selfish to keep their children and that they should not revoke consent to adoption. Some said that until the phone-in they had never known that they could have changed their minds. Their anger and distress at this new information was palpable.

Harri and Ann had thought they might get a half a dozen calls during the phone-in. They got nearly 300.

'We were feeling hysterical when it was over,' Harri said. 'The whole thing was dramatic and gut-wrenching and we knew we had uncovered a profound underground issue that couldn't be ignored any longer.'

It was clear that mothers in South Australia had the same issues as those involved in ARMS interstate. The long silence had finally been broken and the respondents to the phone-in, with the safeguard of anonymity, had taken the opportunity to name the horror of their experience, and to be heard. And above all they needed to talk.

As Harri and Ann locked the Women's Information Switchboard door for the last time they were already planning their next step – to arrange a public meeting while the phone-in response was still fresh in everyone's minds.

3

'Welcome, mothers. Yes, you are mothers'

THE MEETING ROOM at WIS filled rapidly and the group ranged from well-dressed ladies carrying suitable handbags to casual cheesecloth-clad women wearing leather sandals. The age range spanned several generations and it was clear that these mothers had come from all walks of life and were as culturally and ethnically diverse as the rest of the country's population. Some of the women had come alone and when they were organised in their seats they sat in silence looking at the floor. Others glanced furtively at the person in the next seat, just to see what she might look like. Some clutched handkerchiefs ready to absorb any rogue tear that might escape during the proceedings. A quiet nervousness filled the jam-packed space.

Harri and Ann took to the stage at the front of the room and smiled into the audience. And then Harri stepped forward and said in a clear, deep voice, 'Welcome, mothers. Yes, you are mothers.'

The women looked at her, staring in disbelief and shock. A few began crying openly. Some had never been called mothers before. The two convenors introduced themselves and explained why they had decided to have a Mother's Day phone-in. They told the women that nearly 300 mothers had rung in and that the overwhelming majority had said the adoption of their babies had been against their wishes. And as the women stifled coughs and held tissues up to running noses Ann said that almost every mother in the phone-in had felt the loss of her child had continued to haunt her every day of her life.

'Respondents,' Harri read, 'either now felt they had been unjustly and inhumanely treated, or they had internalised the attitudes of others toward them and acted as though they deserved it.'

Heads nodded and women started looking at one another whispering, 'That happened to me. That's how I felt.'

The sameness of experiences among women who had never met one another was tragically obvious and the mothers, at first bewildered, began to realise the enormity of what had happened to them and just how many of them there actually were. They were yet to find out that thousands of other women around Australia had played a role in exactly the same story.

After the business of the meeting was done and it was decided that an ARMS group would be established in Adelaide, an elderly, frail-looking lady with crimped grey hair struggled to her feet. Grabbing a chair to steady herself she turned around and called out, 'Oh my gosh, you are all such lovely ladies.' Croaking with age and suppressed tears, the woman's voice gave away her surprise – and her relief. The women around her smiled. They knew exactly what she meant because they had all felt the same thing themselves. These mothers were not the *bad girls* the women had thought they would see at the meeting, and they were not crazy people who belonged in a mental hospital. These were everyday women who had loved their babies and who had been vilified for doing the very thing that society had demanded of them.

And as the women looked at one another they saw what the old lady had seen, and they realised that if everyone else there was normal then they probably were too. It was the first time they had dared to believe that they might be nice people.

ARMS South Australia was born at that meeting. And as the mothers were sharing names and phone numbers they were also beginning a journey that would change them forever. They would find kindred spirits in unexpected places, and they would battle fierce prejudice and blatant vested interest. And while they were supporting one another and lobbying for change, each and every one of them would have to face the loss of her own baby and deal with the reality of what life would be like now, with or without a reunion with her grown-up child – a child who was a complete stranger.

It would not be an easy road.

4

Forming a Management Committee

NOT ALL WOMEN at the public meeting wanted to become active members of a support group for mothers who had given up their children for adoption. Some were still scared and secretive and they asked to be kept informed through a third person or by a quick telephone call when no one else was at home. It was a tricky business but if anyone knew the importance of secrecy it was those in the ARMS support group. Confidentiality was an absolute priority and everyone understood that to betray another mother's trust was also a betrayal of themselves and everything that ARMS stood for.

The early meetings were held in various locations, and Ann used her social work placement to help the group get established. There was a constitution to be put together and an association to be registered. And most important of all the support group needed an official name.

South Australia decided to take a slightly different name from its sister organisations interstate who were now calling themselves the Association of Relinquishing Mothers. The women called the Adelaide group by the original name, the Australian Relinquishing Mothers Society. They wanted to keep the acronym because they liked the notions of *empty* ARMS and *open* ARMS. Someone mentioned *taking up* ARMS against those people who perpetuated the myth that adopted children had been abandoned by their mothers. The group laughed but decided that it might be just a bit too militant. After all, they had always been portrayed as unfit mothers and the last thing they wanted now was to look like a bunch of gun-toting loonies!

One of ARMS's first members was a mother who had been part of the Jigsaw group who had been meeting in Adelaide well before the 1982 Adoption Conference. Loryn had not telephoned during the phone-in but she heard about Harri and Ann's public meeting from a news item and she decided to go just in case there might be one or two more women she could talk to. She could not believe her eyes when she walked through the door at the WIS meeting and saw the room packed with mothers just like herself.

Gillian had also been at the large meeting after the phone-in. She had felt liberated when she heard the other mothers' stories – it was good to know that she was no longer alone. And she remembered seeing the old woman stand up and speak.

'She must have been in her late seventies and it was the first time she had ever talked about losing her baby,' Gillian said. 'She just cried and cried and I was determined I wasn't going to wait until I was that age before I started talking about what had happened to me.'

Ineke also helped establish ARMS. She had never told anyone about the baby she had adopted out in New South Wales. When she heard on the radio that she could ring someone and talk about it she wrote down the number and waited impatiently for the phone lines to open. Weeks later, when she walked into the large public meeting and saw ninety other mothers, a curious and confronting thing happened to her. 'A woman I knew through a relative came out of the crowd and waved hello,' Ineke said. 'At first I felt a bit apprehensive about approaching her but then I realised that if she was there she must be a relinquishing mother too. She was a likable lady and I thought to myself that if she wasn't a bad person then I couldn't be that bad either. It was a really strange feeling.'

It was Ineke's first experience seeing a mirror image of herself – of realising that mothers were just like everyone else. In that one instant the myth about mothers who gave up children for adoption was exorcised and a huge weight was lifted from Ineke's mind. And although she would still have many feelings about losing her daughter, shame would no longer be one of them.

Valma came to ARMS very early as well. She was a little older than some of the other women and she had kept her baby's adoption a secret longer than many. She was deeply afraid of what would happen if people knew about her past but at the same time she felt compelled to come along and meet these other women who had shared her experience. She remembered the overwhelming feelings that welled up inside her when Harri said, 'Welcome, mothers.'

'After I got married I never had any more children,' Valma said. 'And when women talked about their pregnancies I used to have to pretend I didn't know what it was like. So being called a mother was something I had never expected to hear. I just sat and sobbed into my hands.'

About twenty mothers attended the first ARMS support group and over a hundred asked to receive ongoing information and newsletters. Some women weren't ready to talk about their experience in a group and others said they hadn't told anyone and needed time to speak to family and friends before they *came out*. Others were simply too afraid to talk about it at all. They thought that if they started crying they might never stop.

Gillian became ARMS founding chairperson and Ineke became the key person in charge of collating names and searching birth notices at the State Library.

Loryn was a good all-rounder on the management committee and she also found the little cottage that would become ARMS office some years later.

Valma was also one of the early movers and shakers and she would lead ARMS in its quest for something that had not been given to mothers anywhere else in Australia.

Sue and Maria were also among the first group of courageous mothers to put their hands up and Harri and Ann stayed in touch to lend support in the same way a mother holds her child's hand until it can stand on its own. And in the not too distant future Ann would come back with a wild idea that would take mothers on a journey they could never have imagined.

5

'Sorry, what did you say?'

TWO WEEKS BEFORE the public meeting at WIS I was sitting in a social work class waiting for the lecture to begin. A fellow student I knew fairly well, and who I knew was a single mother, leaned across and started chatting about a phone-in two of her friends had held recently. It was to see if women whose children had been adopted out had any issues around giving up their babies.

'They got hundreds of calls,' the student said. 'And nearly all of them were from women who said they had been pressured into adoption.' I could feel my stomach start to churn.

I had told most of my social work colleagues, including her, that I was the mother of one child, a daughter. It was my standard reply to the 'do you have any children?' question. But it was a lie. And it would take a lot more than a casual friendship for me to be able to tell the whole story about my other child who was born the day after my nineteenth birthday and who I had only seen for two minutes before she was taken away. It was a story that had to be shared in private and there could be no shortcuts, as there was always a lot riding on how well I told it. I had never wanted to give my baby up for adoption and I needed to see that look of understanding in the faces of anyone I told. And, more importantly, I needed to tell it in a way that I did not see that other unmistakable look – the one that said 'I had no idea you were *that kind of girl*. I could *never* have given up my own child. Not under any circumstances'.

I had also found it especially hard to tell my story to single mothers. They had always been a bit of an enigma to me and I felt envious of them and just slightly pathetic in their company. I could never quite work out how they got to keep their children when I did not. Had they known something I did not know, or was I just weak-willed and gave in too easily to the pressure? In any event it was especially hard finding the right time and place to tell someone who had kept her baby that I had given mine to strangers.

It was with this monologue running around in my head that I heard the student say her friends Harri and Ann were holding a public meeting to gather the relinquishing mothers together and that they needed someone who could type up some flyers to put around the university campus.

'Sorry, what did you say?' I asked, feeling something between wanting to vomit and thinking I was going to pass out. The woman went over her story again and I made up my mind that it was time to confess my own experience. Despite my feelings of terror I desperately wanted to know about all these other women who had rung in and I was intrigued about just how many of us were out there. I had thought I was the only one.

Over lunch I told the student about my pregnancy in 1968; how a nurse had held my head down during the delivery so I could not see my baby being born and that the only thing I could look at was the clock, which read half past two. My mouth was dry and my speech was rapid when I said how I had asked to see my little girl and been told it was not allowed. And that after days of asking, someone let me see her for two minutes and that she had curled her little fingers around my own.

I did not look up until I had finished telling my story and when it was done I felt drained and vulnerable. I was always left with that uneasy feeling of wondering if I had told enough of what happened for the person to really know what it was like. Did they really understand the immense pressure on me to give my baby up? Did I remember to tell them that my mother would not let me come home and I had nowhere to go and no way of supporting my baby? Could anyone really understand how I was browbeaten into believing I would be the most selfish person on earth to keep my baby – after all, I had already put shame on my family by becoming pregnant.

The woman touched my hand and told me that the only difference between the two of us was that her mother helped her and she had a home to go to after she had her baby. I knew she understood and I felt relief, and I wanted to cry.

The conversation turned to the phone-in and my new friend told me how callers had talked about being tied down during delivery and that some said they were given a general anaesthetic so they could not see their babies being born. The vast majority of mothers said they had been told they would soon put the experience behind them and get on with their lives. None of them had.

By the end of the lunch break I was so overwhelmed I could not listen to any more and we decided to concentrate on more practical matters. I told my friend I would be happy to type up the flyers and that I would definitely be at the meeting at WIS.

As the day of the meeting grew closer I became more and more paralysed with fear at the thought of being in a room with other mothers. I did not know what they were going to be like. Along with many other people I had swallowed the myth about what kind of woman would give up a baby. I was genuinely afraid of them – even though I was one of them! More than that, I simply could not cope with my own feelings. They had been pent up for so long I did not even really know what they were any more and I had no idea what would happen if I unleashed them. And when I did let them out I was not sure I wanted it to be in public with lots of other women doing the same thing. I decided not to go. And as history would have it I missed an experience that would mark the beginning of ARMS in South Australia and that no one who was there would ever forget.

Fortunately for me my social work friend had put my name on the mailing list of 'interested mothers' after the public meeting, and when the first ARMS newsletter came out I got one. The newsletters came to my home for the next two years before I plucked up the courage and opened one.

The newsletter always came in a plain envelope – (they were

called secret envelopes because they did not give away their contents) but inside there was no mistaking what this literature was about. On the front of the folded pages was a black silhouette of a woman, and in her arms silhouetted in white was the shape of a baby. The absent baby in a mother's arms. It was the perfect logo.

Valma, who was now chairperson, was asking for volunteer counsellors to help work with the increasing number of mothers who were contacting ARMS. The more publicity the support group got, the more people rang in saying they needed to talk about what had happened to them. Valma and the management committee simply could not keep up.

I looked at the advertisement and decided that as I was both a relinquishing mother and a social work student I would be the perfect person to counsel these women. My arrogance was awe-inspiring! I had barely spoken about my experience to anyone else and yet I believed I had what it took to sort out any adoption issue a mother might raise.

I rang Valma expecting that she would be ecstatic to hear from someone like me and so I was more than a little unnerved when she suggested that I should come to a support group meeting first. It did not take me long to work out that this was an astute woman who was not about to let me loose on a group of vulnerable mothers until she knew exactly who I was and what I was like. And she already suspected I might not be as cool about my own experience as I had been letting her think I was.

And of course, as she had predicted, I went to my first meeting and bawled my eyes out. I was not a social work student, or a counsellor. I was a mother and I had just met this amazing bunch of women who were about to change my life.

6

Coming Out

BY THE TIME I joined ARMS things were ticking along fairly well. The organisation was as poor as a church mouse but it did find support from a couple of politicians who paid the postage for the hundred or so newsletters that went out every other month. The Women's Information Switchboard had also allowed ARMS to have its monthly support groups in the main room. It was a great location because it was in a well-lit spot in the centre of the city and women could get there relatively easily from most places around metropolitan Adelaide. Country women, unfortunately, still had to rely on newsletters and very expensive telephone calls for their support. In those days there were no mobile phones, internet connections or telecommunications packages to enable country people to make cheap phone calls around Australia.

In the 1980s it seemed to be the done thing for everyone in a support group to sit around in a circle to talk about how things were going for them. ARMS followed the rule and each mother would take her turn in saying what it had been like to lose her baby and how she needed to know if her child was at least still alive and happy with its new life and parents.

The issue about the child's mortality appeared to be a pretty basic question and after it had come up at several more meetings ARMS decided to write to the Department for Community Welfare's Adoption Services Branch and ask if mothers could be told if their children were still living. The Department had been aware for some time that this was a genuine concern for mothers and it agreed to give the request some consideration. In the meantime meetings at WIS went on as usual. That is, until the night someone forgot the key.

Valma arrived for the support group meeting with her briefcase bulging with papers and news clippings as usual. However, when she walked into the lobby of the main building she found everyone sitting on the steps looking disgruntled. No one had been able to get into the meeting room.

After many accusations about who was supposed to have the key and discussion of what to do about the meeting, someone suggested that it was a nice balmy night and perhaps the group could sit on the lawn next to the War Memorial across the road.

Still mumbling about who was on the roster to pick up the key that night, everyone filed out and congregated on the grass by the Memorial. But there was a problem. In the 1980s there was an unofficial and quite particular ARMS dress code. Mothers dressed up to attend support meetings in defiance of the stereotype of the relinquishing mother wearing tracksuit pants with cigarette burns and spaghetti stains down her terry-towelling top.

It was not long before everyone realised how conspicuous they looked sitting on the War Memorial lawn at 8.30 at night in their finery, and that they would draw even more attention if they formed the obligatory circle to conduct the meeting. Someone suggested a good restaurant on the other side of North Terrace where they could sit and have coffee and cake.

The mothers looked at one another, certain that the meeting would now be out of the question but at least they could talk about regular, non-adoption matters over a bite to eat. And so they brushed the grass off their neat clothes and walked to the brightly lit restaurant with its flashy bay windows and Thai silk curtains.

The first person to mention the adoption word might have been the woman who suggested the restaurant – no one really remembers. But they do know they all froze. Were they really going to talk about their babies in such a public place? What would happen if the people at the next table heard them and realised they were a group of mothers who had given their children up for adoption?

Nevertheless, and in spite of their terrors, they began to chatter. And spurred on by safety in numbers, and an insatiable need to talk about their lost children, they kept on going, sharing a little something about life without their babies. One woman said she had met someone keen to attend the next meeting. Another said she thought she might have found her son. And Valma talked about her conversations with the interstate ARMS groups and what they were doing to try and get more information for mothers. By the end of the evening everyone was talking freely about ARMS topics. There was even some laughter. No one was concerned about what anyone else in the restaurant might be thinking. It might have been empty for all they cared.

As the mothers left they knew something really important had just happened. They had left their safe circle and ventured across the road to a public place. They had said the word adoption and that they were mothers, and they had talked in normal voices – not whispered. It was a special moment for all of them, and for ARMS as an organisation. The mothers had begun 'coming out' and they were doing it as a unified group.

The mothers never did find out who was supposed to open the door to the meeting room that night. But nearly thirty years later everyone there remembers vividly the liberated feeling it gave them when they had their first meeting in public, and they were glad the key had been forgotten.

Other important business happened that month. Adoption Services agreed to do death searches so women could know if their children were still alive, and it would not be long before the inevitable happened.

7

A Death in the Family

BY THE LATE 1970s Adoption Services staff were getting enough requests from mothers and children wanting to meet one another to warrant the suggestion of a contact register. The idea was that both the mother and the adult adoptee over eighteen years of age would have to be registered for a contact to be facilitated by Adoption Services. The father could register if he was on the original birth certificate or if the mother gave her permission.

The register was implemented and although the initiative was welcomed by ARMS and Jigsaw, advertising it to the public was not allowed after the initial press release. Consequently only a couple of hundred contacts occurred in its ten years of operation. What its existence did show, however, was that the Department was beginning to think that contact between consenting adults was not out of the question, and it was starting to listen to what mothers had been saying about losing their babies.

Nonetheless, it was still a surprise and a bit of a coup when Adoption Services announced that it would do a search of South Australian death records on request by a mother or an adult adoptee, and if no death had been registered the person wanting the information would be told. It did not prove that the person had not died interstate – but it was a start.

Some mothers said they did not want a death search done. They had received snippets of non-identifying information from Adoption Services – generally a letter saying what kind of house the baby had gone to and that at the time of adoption the parents and child were happy. The idea of having thought about their children for so long only to find out they had died years earlier was more than they could contemplate. Others said they simply had to know one way or another and they made the most of the opportunity and put in a request.

Early one morning Valma got a call from an extremely distressed woman. She had just left Adoption Services with the worst possible news and she did not know where to turn next. Margaret did not belong to ARMS but she had been very public about her desire to find her daughter over the years. She had appeared in newspapers and magazines and she had even made a plea on national television to anyone who might know the whereabouts of the child she lost thirty-five years ago when she was sixteen years old. When she heard that death searches could be done she applied immediately and waited expectantly for the usual written notification saying that no death had been recorded. However, instead of receiving a letter Margaret was contacted and asked to come in to see a social worker in the Adoption Services Department.

When Margaret met with the staff member she was told that a death search had shown that her daughter had died in a car crash when she was fifteen years old. Worse still, the Department could not tell Margaret her daughter's name or where she was buried because the adoptive mother who had only adopted the one child, and was now a widow, was refusing to allow the information to be divulged. Without the adoptive mother's permission the Department said that all it could do was give Margaret non-identifying information about her daughter's brief life.

Margaret was shattered. She went to the State Library in the hope that she might learn her daughter's name by finding an old newspaper cutting describing a car accident involving a fifteen-year-old girl. She also took her story to the press in the hope that someone might know something, and to highlight what she and ARMS considered were inhumane laws and policies around access to information.

Margaret's tragic story was splashed across the daily paper and among the readers were people who knew the child she was talking about. They contacted her and told her the name of her daughter and where she was buried. It was a tragic end to a mother's search and the only consolation was that Margaret could now at least go to the grave and begin grieving the death of her child who had died twenty years earlier.

A few years later Margaret contacted ARMS with news. The adoptive mother had recently died and had left all her daughter's things to a neighbour who had no interest in them. Knowing the full story, the neighbour got a message to Margaret through the people who had first contacted her, and said that Margaret could come and pick up anything she might want. She went to the house and came away with photos, school memorabilia, trinkets, and artwork her daughter had done. One picture was particularly poignant. It was an oil painting of a girl with a solitary tear falling down her cheek.

Adoption Services' plan to do death searches had been well-intentioned but the Department had not thought through what would happen if someone found out their child had died, particularly where one mother desperately needed the information and the other mother could not cope with parting with it. The Department had to choose between two grieving mothers and although ARMS had some sympathy for the adoptive mother who had to face the loss of her daughter all over again it was nonetheless affronted when the Department chose the wishes of the legal parent over the mother who had had so little for so long.

Adoption Services stopped doing death searches after Margaret's experience. Instead it encouraged applicants, and ARMS, to lobby the government for a review into the State's adoption legislation.

The time had come for ARMS to stand up and be counted as a political force fighting for the rights of mothers whose children had been lost to adoption. But in order to be public it needed a mother who was prepared to be spokesperson; someone who could use newspapers, radio and television effectively to state the mothers' case coherently and rationally; someone who wasn't afraid to tell her own story to the broader population; and someone who could answer the tough questions when they came – and come they would.

ARMS had had spokeswomen before but no one was keen to take on the job. When the current spokesperson left the role often remained vacant until necessity required someone to do it on the hop. Mothers had come a long way but the stigma of motherhood with an adoption tag on the end of it was raw and painful. Shame and acute embarrassment were still part and parcel of the experience and it was a challenge for women to tell the world that they were relinquishing mothers. They had only just begun acknowledging it to themselves.

8

Sophie and Margaret Do Talkback Radio

TALKBACK RADIO WAS IN ITS PRIME in the 1980s and it was a good medium for getting one's point across – that is if you could deal with the people who might ring in and ask curly questions you could not answer.

Valma agreed to be ARMS spokesperson and she nominated me to be ARMS backup *as required*. Our first joint venture came fairly quickly with the offer to be on a talkback radio program dealing with that still emotive issue, unmarried motherhood. It was too good an opportunity to knock back but Valma and I had a serious problem. We were still far too scared to use our real names in the media, especially if we were going to be required to talk about ourselves as mothers who were not only single during pregnancy but who had not kept our babies. We knew it was cowardly but we agreed to use false names. She would be called Sophie and I would be Margaret.

We arrived at the radio station and were efficiently ushered into a studio very like the one used by the talkback psychiatrist in the television series *Frasier*. The desk was covered in switches and microphones and the program compere, a minister of the cloth, introduced himself and urged us not to worry, everything would be fine. I did not feel at all fine. My legs were shaking and I desperately wanted to go to the bathroom. I turned towards Valma sitting next to me and she looked like the proverbial deer caught in the headlights. The look of terror on her face was not at all consoling.

The program format was straightforward. The compere would

ask us to tell the listeners why we had chosen adoption as the solution to unwed pregnancy, and after describing our experiences we would take calls from anyone who rang in. There was a twelve-second delay on telephone calls to the radio station so any belligerent listeners would be cut off before they got to air. But as it turned out a caller behaving badly was not going to be our main issue.

Neither Valma nor I had ever talked about ourselves on air before and we were not doing a particularly good job at it now. My mouth was parched and I was speaking so fast I sounded like a runaway train. I could not find the words to describe my own experience, and my reasons for giving up my child seemed hollow and self-interested. Valma was not doing much better than me, and between the two of us we bumbled our way through five minutes of pure hell. And then the calls started coming in!

An angry-sounding man rang in and said that he thought adoption by a married couple was better than single motherhood and that, in his opinion, abortion was absolutely out of the question. Valma and I looked at one another, clenched our teeth and said that we understood that for some children adoption might have been a good thing but that for others it had left them with feelings of abandonment and rejection. Valma added that for the mother it left a lifelong feeling of emptiness and loss. We did not respond to the abortion remark. It was not a debate ARMS had ever wanted to weigh into. It knew that if it did the inevitable question from the anti-abortion lobby would be 'Are you saying that it would have been better for your baby to be killed rather than give it to people who would love it?' It was a question ARMS would never be able to answer.

Next we heard a familiar voice. It was Harrison ringing to offer support and to ask a pertinent question that would allow us to impart words of wisdom upon the listeners – except that neither of us understood what she wanted us to say.

Harrison began by talking about the negative aspects of adoption and then she went on to ask if we thought that life had been difficult for single women who had kept their babies as well. She was wanting us to make the valid point that unmarried mothers who kept their children also suffered from the stigma of unwed pregnancy, and that pensions, childcare, and job opportunities for single mothers in the 1980s were still appallingly inadequate.

The problem was that Valma and I had not yet sorted the issue out in our own heads. We saw single mothers as being the lucky ones – the women who had, somehow, been allowed to keep their babies. Frankly, we were jealous of them. And the notion that they might be suffering some of the same prejudices we had endured eluded us entirely. And so when Harrison asked if we thought single mothers were as badly off as relinquishing mothers I, shamefully, said no.

Harri's silence echoed in my ears and I could hear her take a deep breath and try to ask the question differently. But neither Valma nor I knew how to answer it any other way. We simply could not imagine that any mother who had been allowed to keep her child could have been as hard done by as us.

Worse than our failure to understand the issues for any girl who became pregnant in those days, we had offended the very woman who had called us 'mothers' for the first time. Without Harri and Ann ARMS would not have become the organisation it was, and here we were saying publicly that Harri and all the single mothers like her had had an easy time of it, whilst we relinquishing mothers were the real victims of an unjust world that made us give up our children to strangers.

After the show I tried to apologise to Harrison but I simply could not explain my behaviour properly. I felt embarrassed and ashamed. And when Valma and I debriefed our first 'on-air' experience, the thing that stood out for us was that we needed to understand more about the similarities between single mothers and relinquishing mothers rather than focus on the differences.

Years later a friend told me that her son was born in 1975 when she was seventeen and single. Her mother was fully supportive of her keeping the baby and she returned home to a loving family ready to help her raise her little boy. For several months, however, the new mother had to take her baby to see a government worker every second week where he would be undressed and inspected for bruises or other signs of neglect. The girl believed that if she did not attend the inspections her baby would be taken from her and it was a fear that haunted her for years. Not only had she suffered the stigma of an unwed pregnancy, she also had to deal with the unfounded belief that unmarried mothers were more likely to hurt their babies than married ones and that the government needed to keep a close eye on them.

I relayed my friend's story to Harri when I finally had the courage to talk about my infamous radio gaffe. She did not remember the incident but she recalled that several times after her own son was born she was visited by two suited men and a woman who would arrive at her home, unannounced, to see her and her baby.

'There was nothing malevolent about them,' she said. 'They just sat around the kitchen table drinking tea. But my gut was in knots. I knew why they were there.'

Being visited by 'the welfare' if you were an unmarried mother was not uncommon and the fear of losing your child was ever-present. And even after the Department stopped coming there was still the possibility that they might return in the future. Harrison's point that single women who kept their children also had a hard time was well-founded. Like relinquishing mothers they were vilified while they were pregnant. However, a relinquishing mother could slip back into anonymity after giving up her baby. The child of a single mother, however, was a constant reminder of the woman's so-called *loose morals* and that, in itself, seemed to justify the Department scrutinising her in case she lapsed back into her past behaviour and placed the child at risk. And, of course, until 1973 single mothers were not eligible for a pension and even after that time the payment was never above the poverty line.

Valma and I often wished we could have had another opportunity to answer Harrison's question about single mothers on talkback radio. Our answer, a second time, would have been vastly different.

The next time on radio I was on my own and I got caught out beautifully. This time I was interviewed by a well-known radio personality and I respected the woman immensely. ARMS brief was that I should talk about the quarter of a million women who had lost children through adoption and that there needed to be an urgent review of adoption legislation to open up secret records. I was there in my capacity as ARMS spokesperson, not to talk about my own experience.

In the warm-up before we went on air the announcer asked the same predictable questions including the one about whether or not I was a relinquishing mother. I answered that I was, but I was there to talk about statistics, laws, policies etcetera and that I did not want to speak about my own experience on radio. I felt confident that she understood the parameters around our interview.

During the broadcast, which was live, the interviewer asked all the right questions allowing me to sprout my statistics and spruik endlessly about the intricacies of adoption legislation in South Australia. And then, clearly aware that she and all her listeners were beginning to nod off, she looked me straight in the eye and said, 'And, Meg, are *you* a relinquishing mother?'

I was not going to lie. Valma and I had only recently decided that if we were going to have any integrity in what we were doing we had to use our own names in any future media interviews, and if we were asked about our own status we would always say that we were relinquishing mothers. We knew that as ambassadors for ARMS we could not tell other women that they had done nothing to be ashamed of if we were too scared to declare ourselves.

'Yes, I am,' I said feeling angry and betrayed.

'And have you met your daughter?' the announcer asked, knowing she was on a winner and that any dozing listener would have perked up by now.

'No,' I answered, trying to sound natural but feeling absolutely furious and quite terrified.

'So, Meg, what would you say to your daughter if you met her?' she asked.

I was still angry. But the woman's question was so close to my heart I could not help but answer it exactly as I would have if it had been my child sitting in front of me.

'I would tell her that I've always loved her and that I never wanted to give her up,' I answered. Interview over.

ARMS and I learned something very useful that day. Be prepared for anything and never assume an interviewer is going to play by *your* rules!

ARMS did some interesting interviews but none was as pleasant, and as dangerous, as the one done over breakfast in a luxurious Adelaide hotel. And this time it was another woman who learned about the traps one can fall into when dealing with the media.

A prominent Adelaide radio station had a popular segment where it interviewed people over breakfast in a restaurant or café. ARMS jumped at the chance to be part of it. Two ARMS members and an adoptive parent would be the guests. The views of the adoptive mother chosen were very different from ARMS. She was totally opposed to any law changes opening secret adoption records but she was a pleasant lady and her presence would make for a balanced discussion.

The interview was set for 8 am and spread out on a crisp linen tablecloth lay a delectable feast of croissants, white and wholemeal toast, fresh fruit and juice, tea and coffee, and conserve and cream. The sound man fitted everyone with small button microphones and over the clinking of cups upon saucers and the crunch of buttered toast the guests started to chat. The ambiance was pampering – and dangerously deceptive. It would be very easy to forget this was a radio interview and say something regrettable. And that is exactly what happened. The adoptive mother began talking about her experience bringing up adopted children and how she loved them all as if they were her own. Unfortunately, she went on to say things that she said were *in confidence* and which she would never tell another living soul. Of course, unwittingly she had just shared her secrets with everyone listening to this particular program, a considerable number.

The ARMS representatives, of whom I was one, had not agreed with very much of what she was saying, but we were concerned that she had not realised that she was divulging confidences all over the place. Our stares and raised eyebrows, however, only spurred her on. She clearly took our looks as signs of disapproval. And the interviewer was, of course, encouraging her to keep going – it was a great interview for the radio station.

After the breakfast was over everyone went their separate ways and when I got back to the ARMS office I rang the lady immediately. I told her what she had inadvertently done and that it was fortunate the program was pre-recorded because she could ask them to edit out where she had been a little indiscrete. The poor woman was devastated and no doubt she called the radio station immediately.

The moral of the story? Be aware of the setting you are being interviewed in, and always beware of program hosts bearing hot coffee and croissants.

9

An Opportunity

BY THE 1980s, Australia's mood had changed considerably when it came to secrecy in adoption – and adoption in general. The number of adopted people demanding the same rights as everyone else in society – that is, the right to know their biological beginnings – was growing quickly. More mothers were joining ARMS and they, Jigsaw and Lila's group, Parents of Adoptees, were lobbying for a review of South Australia's adoption legislation. There was general agreement that secrecy in adoption had been a failure and that records should be opened. The question was, to whom?

In 1984 Victoria became the first State in Australia to change its adoption laws and open up past secret records to adopted people over the age of eighteen. Mothers and fathers were not given the same rights, although they could ask the Department for Community Services to make an approach to the family of the adoptee. However, if the adoptive parents did not want information given out it would not be.

New South Wales was now in the process of reviewing its own legislation. Sue Vardon had been Director of Operations with the Department for Youth and Community Services in New South Wales when it was drafting its new Adoption Bill. In 1985 she was brought to South Australia to become Director-General for Community Welfare, working under Greg Crafter who was at that time Minister for Community Welfare. The new Director-General mentioned that Victoria had radically changed its adoption legislation and New South Wales was working on a similar new Bill.

In light of a dramatic shift in thinking on adoption, Sue Vardon believed it might be time for South Australia to seriously consider its own adoption laws.

Wherever proposed adoption law changes had been debated interstate there was divided opinion. Many were in favour of giving adopted adults access to their birth records but there was an equally vocal group who believed that the status quo of total secrecy should be maintained. ARMS in Victoria had not succeeded in getting rights for mothers when that State's laws were passed, and New South Wales was grappling with similar issues. There had been no major political debate on adoption reform in South Australia, and now suddenly the topic was on the government's doorstep and it had to find out the public's views on the matter. The Minister asked Women's Adviser Rosemary Wighton if she would become Deputy Director-General and head the research and community consultation process, and then work with the Crown Solicitor in drafting the new Adoption Bill.

Rosemary worked tirelessly over the next months, into years, to ensure that all the interest groups were heard. She met with government and non-government agencies, ARMS, Jigsaw, Parents of Adoptees, adoptive parents groups, Aboriginal community groups and individuals who all had an opinion on what should be included – and excluded – from any new adoption legislation. Every group had its own opinions and not all of their suggestions were compatible with one another.

The issue of mothers being allowed to apply for identifying information was often at the centre of the debate, but Rosemary, former Women's Adviser to the South Australian Government, was a feminist. There was no doubt in her mind that mothers should be afforded the same rights as adopted people. It was not, however, a view that was shared by everyone.

At the beginning of 1987, Adoption Services released its Review Committee's report on what it believed South Australia's new adoption laws should include. Following Victoria's lead, it recommended that adoptees over the age of eighteen should be entitled to their original birth certificates, identifying their mothers, and fathers if they were on the certificate, without restriction. The review did not support mothers or fathers having identifying information but it did say they could ask Adoption Services to approach the adopted adult on their behalf. If the adopted person said no, however, that would be the end of it. The recommendations were an improvement on the old legislation, and on Victoria's requirement that any Departmental approach would be made through the adoptive parents regardless of the adoptee's age, but it was clearly not equitable and ARMS was bitterly offended.

In order to find out what the general community thought of its proposals, Adoption Services advertised that it would be conducting a phone-in and all interested parties were encouraged to make their views known. ARMS responded with a lengthy press release stating its many concerns about the recommendations, a key one being that there was no requirement to tell the mother if her child's adoption had broken down or if it had not taken place at all. This, ARMS believed, was unacceptable. ARMS approved of Adoption Services recommendations about openness in future adoptions. However, it remained annoyed that the mothers who were suffering the consequences of past adoptions still did not seem to be recognised as deserving the same right to apply for identifying information as their children. ARMS knew it needed to become more political.

ARMS had surpassed anything it could have possibly envisaged in its early days. It was a support service for mothers but now it also had a firm grasp on broader issues to do with adoption and it was developing a credible public voice. It had strong links with its sister groups interstate and they were sharing knowledge and strategies about support, community education and politicking for legislative change. But ARMS also knew that if it was going to get equal rights for mothers in the new laws, it was going to have to campaign long and hard. And so when I was offered the opportunity to do my final year social work placement at ARMS I was ecstatic. I just was not sure where Valma was going to put my desk!

South Australia had had several politically progressive

governments during the 1970s and 1980s and there was a strong bi-partisan commitment to addressing a range of social justice issues. Working in partnership with the non-government sector to meet the needs of newly identified vulnerable groups was high on the agenda of Labor's Bannon Government and the Non-Government Welfare Unit was established with this in mind. Many issues were on the table for consideration and adoption had not passed by without notice. This was fortunate because Valma was about to make a cheeky request.

ARMS was still running its office from Valma's home and apart from it being a long way out of town her house was small and not very conducive to running a busy counselling service, much less housing a social work student and all her stuff. It was for reasons of space and accessibility that ARMS had been having its support meetings at WIS for some years. But there was no space for me there either. I tried not to worry about it but I was more than relieved, and just a little stunned, when Valma rang and told me she had found me a desk and a phone slap bang in the middle of the Non-Government Welfare Unit in the city – the place that handed out all the funding to genuine groups in need, just like ARMS! And ARMS certainly needed money.

ARMS had been running on a shoestring for years. A benefactor was paying the postage on the newsletters and somewhere along the line Valma had scrounged a second-hand photocopier and a dilapidated typewriter. But the Holy Grail was certainly getting government funding to run a service where women could meet and counselling could be provided in a central location. ARMS needed a trained counsellor and it also needed an administrator to handle the increasing paperwork and phone calls. But its submissions had always been knocked back. No adoption support group in Australia, much less South Australia, had ever been able to get government funding of the calibre that ARMS wanted, and a social work placement based in the Non-Government Welfare Unit provided the perfect opportunity for me to raise ARMS's profile and, naturally discretely, state its case.

Peter Bicknell, who managed the Unit, was a social worker who had been involved in overseeing the adoptions of the children and babies who came to Australia as part of the Operation Babylift initiative after the fall of Saigon at the end of the Vietnam War in 1975. It had been a chaotic time and there were fears that if the so-called orphaned children were not taken out of Vietnam immediately they would be killed by the North Vietnamese. Years later some of those children, now grown up, would argue that their lives were never in danger and that they should not have been taken away from their country and culture. Peter remained of the view that the government at the time was acting in what it believed was the best interest of those children.

The Non-Government Welfare Unit was housed in a large open-planned building and Peter and his staff were pleasant and accommodating. I felt a bit guilty about bombarding them with tales of woe about ARMS financial situation and I am sure everyone knew my agenda was to make them *want* to fund the group. Nevertheless I continued, and when I was on the phone I would speak as loudly as permissible so that everyone could hear how busy ARMS was and that it was dealing with critical issues.

One day Peter quietly sidled up next to my desk and asked me very politely if I would mind keeping my voice down just a little because there were no internal walls in the place and everyone could hear what I was saying. Realising that this was the end of my 'say it out as loud as you can' strategy I turned my attention to getting to know the staff of the Unit individually and telling them all about my placement. I thought I was being terribly clever.

Some years later Peter told me that I could have saved my breath – and my voice. ARMS had been on the government's radar for some time and it was well within the brief of the Non-Government Welfare Unit to provide support to mothers by giving a student access to its facilities during her placement. It was one of the strategies the Unit regularly employed to help budding agencies get up and running, and it was already considering giving ARMS seeding funding to get properly established.

My presence in the Unit did not particularly influence the government's ultimate decision to fund ARMS the following year. I was nonetheless very grateful to be given a spot in the Unit and I learned a lot about how non-government organisations got funding to keep their services going. It turned out to be a productive and enlightening social work placement and it gave me, and ARMS, some valuable insights into how different governments operated – and how to write a funding submission properly.

10

A Mother's Story

PAMELA HAD BEEN IN DENIAL about her pregnancy for the better part of its first six months. It was 1961 and she was nineteen years old and single. Her parents were conservative and highly strung and she knew they would not accept her being *in the family way*. It was something she was struggling with herself.

When seven months pregnant and no longer able to disguise the lump beneath her conveniently smocked work uniform, she decided she would leave home, have the baby and raise it on her own. She had read an article advertising a number of unmarried mothers' homes where young single girls could stay until their babies were born and she decided to move into one of them so she could get the help and support she was going to need during the next few months.

Pamela had no intention of giving up her child and she chose a home from her own faith, secure in the belief that people from her religious persuasion would be sympathetic to her situation and that despite them also arranging adoptions they would help her keep her baby. She packed a small suitcase, handed her mother a letter telling her she was pregnant and where she was going, and left.

Pamela was pleasantly surprised when she saw the outside of the unmarried mothers' home. The building did not look like an institution, more like an ordinary home, only much larger. It had a low fence at the front, and roses dotted around a tidy lawn. The old bluestone house nestled among other quality homes in a leafy suburb and at first glance no one would ever know that anything untoward was going on behind its locked doors.

Once inside, the home was not quite as impressive. The sleeping quarters comprised one long dormitory containing twenty single iron-framed beds, ten on either side of a wide walkway, and each with its standard saggy flock mattress and tatty chenille bedspread. Next to each bed was a small cabinet, some grey steel like the ones used in hospitals, others scratched pieces of wooden bric-a-brac. Nothing matched and there was a sense that everything in the room had been donated by good Christian families or hospitals upgrading their furniture.

The kitchen was large and looked like it was the hub of the home. A chrome-framed laminate table stood in the middle of the room with a huddle of chairs scattered around it. The cupboards extended to the twelve-foot-high ceiling. On the kitchen bench sat a tin tea caddy and an opened packet of drinking chocolate. Two large stoves covered in battered pans and kettles stood at one end of the room and a noisy refrigerator chugged away in the corner.

Across the hall was a dreary sitting room with a worn carpet square in its centre. Mismatched and badly sprung chairs hugged the walls giving little warmth to the large room.

Through the window Pamela could see outside to the back of the property. It was an old-fashioned garden of fruit trees, stubbly grass and vegetable patches, and in one corner stood a small shed-like structure called the Chapel. Here the girls were expected to spend time each day in prayer for their sins.

The boundary at the back of the home was defined by a high wrought-iron fence with spikes along the tops of each elaborate metal rung. The paths leading to the front garden had been blocked off years before and the only way anyone could get to the street was through the house itself.

Separated from the main building, but joined to it by a covered walkway, was a large louvred room where the babies stayed. Inside were a couple of cream painted iron cots and a dozen or so bassinets on sturdy stands. There was the usual assortment of unmatched cupboards and chairs and a single bed that stood at the far end of the room. Pamela was heartened by the gurgling sounds coming from the bassinets and the little hands and faces poking up from under fluffy blankets. Clearly this was a place that supported young mothers keeping their babies. Otherwise why would they be here?

Within days Pamela learned the truth about the home she was going to live in for the next few months. The front yard with its roses and low fence was off limits. The girls were only allowed into the backyard and they were never to go off the premises unsupervised. They had to start work straight away, no matter how advanced their pregnancies were. Duties included scrubbing floors, washing and cleaning, and the girls were expected to resume these responsibilities as soon as they came back to the home after giving birth. Worst of all, the babies were in the separate building because they were all being adopted. They were kept away from the main house because it was considered undesirable for the new mothers to spend non-essential time with their newborns. Only one girl was allowed to take care of the infants and she slept in the nursery. It was her job to make sure the breastfed babies were taken to their respective mothers and returned immediately after feeding. She did the bottle feeding herself and took care of all the babies' daily needs including scrubbing the concrete floor and keeping the nursery spotless. Most importantly, she had to make sure the mothers did not sneak into the nursery and play with their babies as such contact was severely frowned upon by Matron.

The work was hard and days were long. Contaminated and bloodied laundry was brought in from a nearby infectious diseases hospital and it was a heavy job lifting the wet sheets and towels out of the industrial washing machines and laying them out on the old steam press for ironing. Equally hard was the task of kneeling on all fours, with a large stomach almost touching the ground, and scrubbing the cold floors of the huge home.

By the end of the day the girls were exhausted and there was not much discussion in the dormitory before lights out. The only person who could not sleep was the girl who spent her nights in the nursery. If she was unlucky enough to be attending to a baby when dinner was served she missed out and she would have to make do with leftovers after the last child was asleep – which would not be for a long time if the nursery was full.

As soon as Pamela was settled into her new quarters Matron called her into the office for the mandatory interview about her background. Matron was a stocky middle-aged woman with a stern face and grey hair pulled back in a severe bun. Her voice, however, was not in keeping with her features and when she talked about the perfect family she had found for Pamela's baby if she had a boy her tone was soft and sweet. She was visibly excited when she said that Pamela's hair and skin colouring, and her well-spoken manner, were an exact match for the couple she had picked out and that a son with her attributes would fit in with the new family extremely well.

It did not take Pamela long to realise that this was not going to be the supportive environment she had imagined. She said nothing about the fact that she would not be giving her baby up to anyone. It was a secret she was going to keep to herself – at least for now.

There were about a dozen girls at the home while Pamela was there and she befriended a young lass who was keeping a similar secret. Her family had told her she could not come home with a baby but she was not ready to consider giving it up for adoption either. The two girls whispered about how they wanted to keep their babies but they did not know how they were actually going to make it happen. Matron was constantly telling them that adoption was their only choice and they knew that simply saying no to her was not going to be enough. And escaping with their newborns would not be simple either. The home was like a fortress and there was always someone on duty. Even when they went to the hospital for their check-ups they were accompanied by one of the staff. The two girls knew that after their babies were born they were never going to be left alone with them long enough to simply walk out the front door with them in their arms.

Throughout the pregnancy Matron regularly met with Pamela to tell her about the importance of giving her baby to people who could afford to give it a good life. She constantly reminded her of the sin and shame of a single pregnancy and that the only way to save the illegitimate child was to let it be adopted by a married couple.

Pamela's silence during these conversations unnerved Matron and as the due date came closer the pressure to consent to adoption became more rigorous. Some nights, exhausted from a long day's work, Pamela would be woken from her sleep and taken to the kitchen where Matron would be waiting with a hot chocolate for them both. Once there she would be subjected to a yawning hour of Matron's views on girls who selfishly wanted to keep their babies, and the virtues of those who made the ultimate sacrifice to give them up. It was obvious to Pamela that Matron was trying to manipulate her while she was tired and vulnerable and she was determined she would never give in.

It was some hours before anyone took Pamela seriously when she finally went into labour. She had told Matron that she thought she was having contractions and was waved off with something for a headache. Each time she came back saying the pain was no better Matron gave her more pills and told her it could not be labour because she was not due for several weeks.

By the time Pamela's waters broke Matron had gone off duty and a more sympathetic staff member called a taxi to take her straight to hospital. Alone and scared, and groggy from headache pills, Pamela climbed into the cab with a bag containing toiletries and headed off into the night.

It was a long and painful labour and after a complicated delivery Pamela gave birth to a healthy little boy. However, instead of staying in hospital to recuperate, she was ushered back to the unmarried mothers' home two days after the birth. The baby, whom she named Anthony, was taken to the nursery and, in spite of having stitches, Pamela was made to resume her scrubbing and cleaning duties the next day.

By a stroke of luck the girl who worked in the nursery had gone home and after a few days Pamela was given the job of looking after all the babies. The hours were long and the work was exhausting but Pamela was happy because she knew that in the nursery she would be able to spend more time cuddling and caring for her own little boy. However, she had not escaped Matron's notice.

Discussions about Anthony began to take on a more unpleasant tone. Emotional blackmail and coercion seemed to dominate Matron's conversations with Pamela. The midnight commands to take hot chocolate with Matron started again and, once she was there, Pamela was reminded about the lovely adoptive parents who had wanted a little boy for such a long time, and how selfish it would be of her not to give her baby to them. It was becoming apparent to Matron that Pamela had plans other than adoption and any gentleness in her manner now gave way to harsh and angry accusations.

Pamela and her friend knew time was running short as Matron grew more suspicious and hostile. Between them they developed a plan to buy two tickets to Sydney where they would rent a flat together. One of them would find work and the other would stay at home and look after the two babies. But they had no idea how to get to the bus depot to buy the tickets, or how they were going to escape from the building without being detected.

As it happened, the unmarried mothers' home was short-staffed on the day Pamela had to go to the hospital for her post-natal check up. Knowing the baby was safely at the home Matron allowed Pamela to go out unsupervised, and making the most of her freedom she detoured past the bus depot and bought two tickets to Sydney. She also bought a bundle of nappies and bunny rugs, which she hid in her bag and folded in amongst the babies' blankets when she got back to the nursery. With the means to get to Sydney, and baby clothes squirrelled away until they needed them, the two girls settled down to plan the day they would escape from what now seemed like a prison.

Several weeks after the secret excursion Pamela's friend took her to one side to tell her some exciting news. Her father, a church minister, had forgiven her. She could bring her baby home after all. The two girls hugged and cried. They were happy that one of them was going to be able to walk out of the building with her child, but they both knew that it was going to be all that much harder for the one remaining. Pamela told her friend that she would still go to Sydney where she would throw herself on the mercy of friends in the hope that they would take pity on her until she found a place for Anthony and herself to live.

The day Pamela was most afraid of finally came. Matron was now insisting that she sign the Consent to Adoption form. Pamela was reminded that a family had already been found for her son and that they could give him a proper education – something she could not guarantee herself – and that it would be irresponsible of her to consider anything other than handing him over. Despite pleas for more time Pamela was marched off to the city where, with an adoption worker standing over her, she signed the papers.

Pamela might have signed the form to give Anthony up for adoption but she had certainly not changed her mind about keeping him. She had tried to convince everyone that she should be allowed to have her baby with her but they just kept saying it was impossible. She hoped that now the form was signed Matron would leave her alone long enough to finalise her escape plan. She knew she did not have long.

Unlike more recent adoption practices where babies were taken at birth and the mother did not see her child at all, this unmarried mothers' home made the new mothers feed their babies for at least two months. Anthony was several weeks old now, alert and healthy. In the safety of the nursery Pamela packed a bag for herself and the baby and waited for the changeover of staff, knowing at this time she would be less likely to be seen leaving. With her bus ticket in her purse and Anthony bundled up in her arms she quietly made her way to the front door.

'Where do you think you are going with that baby?' a voice boomed. Someone had told Matron that Pamela was planning to escape with her son and the woman was lying in wait for her. Pamela told Matron that she was taking her baby and leaving; Anthony was her son and she was not giving him to anyone. Matron straightened her back and yelled that if Pamela dared to take the baby off the premises the police would be called and she would sent to gaol for stealing.

Pamela stood welded to the spot as Matron reminded her that the adoption papers had been signed and the baby no longer belonged to her. And as quickly as the tirade had commenced it stopped. Matron smiled at Pamela and told her that if she was a good girl and took Anthony back to the nursery straight away the matter would be forgotten and she would be allowed to look after him until his parents picked him up two weeks later. If she continued with her current plan, however, the baby would be taken from her right now and it would be the last time she would see him.

Pamela felt utterly defeated. She believed that if she tried to leave she would be arrested and she would never see Anthony again. At least if she did what Matron wanted she would have him for a little longer. She returned to the nursery with Anthony and two weeks later she dressed him in the clothes the adoptive parents had sent in and handed him to Matron. She never saw her baby again.

With the passage of time Pamela, like many other mothers, began to feel guilty about giving up her son. Despite the obvious pressure she had been placed under by the unmarried mothers' home, and by her family and society in general, she had taken on the shame and guilt falsely associated with single pregnancy and adoption. She became silent and secretive and those feelings, along with sadness, grief and anger, stayed deep inside her.

Pamela joined ARMS in 1983 and when she retold her story for *Mothers in ARMS* she started crying. 'I felt totally broken,' she said. 'I tried so hard to keep my baby and in the end there was just no way out. What makes it worse is that I never knew until I joined ARMS that I could have changed my mind at any time up until my baby was taken by the adoptive parents. In the whole time I was there they never mentioned it once. And when I signed the consent form the adoptions worker didn't tell me either.' Her voice turned to anger as she added, 'I could have walked out with my baby and they could not have stopped me. The Matron told me I would be arrested. It was a blatant lie. How could people from a church home behave like that?'

In years to come ARMS would hear many stories like Pamela's and it would become obvious that these consents were invalid on several counts. Firstly, it was illegal to gain a consent under duress. Second, failing to inform a mother of her right to revoke consent also invalidated the consent. Third, a consent was not legal if the mother was not fully informed about what it meant to give consent to adoption. And ARMS would uncover evidence to suggest that the consent forms themselves were wrongly worded and that mothers were misled about what a consent to adoption really meant.

Pamela did not see her baby again but she did meet her son as an adult. He had been given a different name and there were many years for them both to catch up on. Now they have a friendship that is shared among their mutual families, their children and grandchildren. Pamela's story has had a good ending but one cannot escape the fact that it should never have happened in the first place.

Mothers' stories are never just their own, and in their telling they can identify and impact upon many other people. Out of respect for her son and his family's privacy Pamela asked that her real name not be used here and that the name she took throughout her stay at the unmarried mothers' home be used instead.

What is important in her story is that in spite of what happened to her and that, like so many other women, she took on a mantle of guilt and shame about giving up her child, she was not bitter and resentful. Her resilience and courage won out. She came to ARMS and campaigned for the rights of mothers and she supported them through their own sadness. In spite of her fear she stood up and exposed the adoption myth by telling her story. And it was that singular determination so evident in ARMS mothers that led the group to succeed so remarkably in the years to come.

11

The Ultimate Betrayal

AS MORE MOTHERS CAME to ARMS, it confirmed that their fears and hopes were the same. They remained overwhelmed about having to give up their babies and the only thing that eased their grief was the belief that their children had been given the happy lives they had been promised. The women clung to the hope that all the people who had told them that adoption was the proper thing – the only thing to do – were right. The doctors, nurses, social workers and almoners who had been the prime movers in promoting adoption had insisted that adoptive parents were all carefully selected and that the babies would be going to married couples who would love and take care of their children in a way the mothers themselves could not. If this did not happen then mothers would have considered it to be the ultimate betrayal.

It hit the papers in mid 1987 – news that a cult had been exposed near Lake Eildon in Victoria, and that children and teenagers had been removed from the property. Rumours had been rife since the 1960s that children were living at the Eildon farm, but the people staying there initially denied it. Eventually the members admitted that young people were there, and after issues were raised around their welfare and educational needs arrangements were made between their guardians, Community Services Victoria and the Education Department for them to be home-schooled on the property. Over the years suspicions remained about the children, all with strange blonde hair, and after a lengthy and substantial police investigation there was enough evidence to justify the removal of the children.

The story was sensational and each day the press revealed more information about the cult's operations. Its leader was Anne Hamilton-Byrne, a charismatic woman who believed she was Jesus reincarnated. She led a group of followers, including doctors, nurses, social workers, lawyers and teachers, who also believed her delusions. Some had met Hamilton-Byrne through a yoga class she was running. Others had been clients or acquaintances of cult members and were talked into meeting the woman with deep mystical qualities who could change their lives.

Most of the cult members spent weekends or holidays at the property but did not live there all the time. They had regular homes in mainstream society, working in their own professions and leading seemingly normal lives. Some never told anyone, other than those they were trying to convert, about their secret passion. Others took their families to the property where the children were supervised by members called 'aunties'. The common theme among them was that they all believed that Hamilton-Byrne had special powers and that she could make those who followed her more fulfilled – and powerful.

The story would have remained a bizarre and remote tragedy to the ARMS mothers had it not been for the fact that Hamilton-Byrne and her cohorts were involved in a sophisticated and long-standing adoption racket. Doctors, nurses and social workers were illegally arranging for babies born to young single mothers to be adopted into the cult. A lawyer cult member falsified birth certificates and after a fraudulent paper trail some of the babies were adopted by Hamilton-Byrne herself, who claimed three of the children were her biological triplets. In reality the babies were born some months apart to different mothers, one of whom gave birth in New Zealand. Information was never released to say exactly how many babies had been taken in the adoption scam that ran from the 1960s to the mid 1970s.

Several ARMS mothers in South Australia had been sent interstate to have their babies – *out of sight out of mind* – and like their sisters in Victoria and the other States, they were horrified by what they heard and terrified about what it might mean. Frantic calls between ARMS groups occurred almost daily but little more was known than the news reported in the daily papers. ARMS rang Community Services Victoria on behalf of its South Australian members who had had their babies in Melbourne but no one was able to convey any useful information. The Department promised to call if anything turned up. It was an agonising wait.

Between twenty and thirty children were alleged to have lived at the Eildon property during the cult's heyday. Some were the children of cult members. Others came to the place as babies, newly adopted through at least one major public hospital in Melbourne where cult members worked and were able to manipulate the adoption system. A lawyer from the cult forged official documents and children's passports. Some children did not know their real dates of birth. Others were unaware they were not Hamilton-Byrne's biological children. There was also speculation that the cult might have been involved in baby trafficking on an international scale. The children experienced significant mental and physical torture and were crammed into a small space under the building and hidden when unexpected visitors arrived. They were not allowed to tell anyone about their lives in the cult and if they did not meet Hamilton-Byrne's strict rules they had their heads held under water until they confessed to their bad behaviour. The children were beaten and starved and given LSD and other experimental drugs. They were frightened of the outside world and were told that strangers were dangerous and would do terrible things if they got hold of them. And in a demented act that had a sick parallel to Hitler's Aryan fantasy, every child who was not fair-haired had his or her hair dyed blonde. Their lives could not have been further from what the mothers had been told their children would experience when they went to their new adoptive families.

Women were already angry with the people who had bullied them into giving up their babies, and the fact that some of these professionals were complicit in a scam to give these babies to someone who believed she was God was the ultimate betrayal. If there had been any trust between mothers and the so-called *helping professions* it was now all but gone. Mothers also worried that if this particular adoption scam was able to exist for so many years who was to say that babies were not being given to other unstable groups or couples. ARMS had already come to believe that the adoption of many babies was illegal, but the thought that the children might have been harmed in their new homes was simply more than the mothers could comprehend.

Worse was the fact that mothers had no legal right to find out what happened to their children. Victoria's laws had only given adopted adults the right to know their parents' names. Mothers and fathers were entirely at the mercy of Community Services Victoria and although the Department was sympathetic, some adoption records had gone missing and there were no guarantees that all the parents of the cult children would be found.

ARMS mothers in Victoria protested in the city streets with placards demanding answers about how the cult could have existed for so long and why the perpetrators of the adoption scam were not arrested. 'Is my child a victim of the Hamilton-Byrne Conspiracy?' one frightened woman wrote. Without any legal rights all the mothers could do was take to the streets to seek answers to their questions.

The media reported that some children were reunited with their parents and one child, Sarah Moore, wrote a book called *Unseen Unheard Unknown* describing her experience as one of Hamilton-Byrne's alleged triplets. I spoke with her recently and she said her mother who was fifteen when Sarah was born, had pillows stacked on her chest so she could not see her baby when it was taken away. In her book Sarah disclosed the identities of some of the doctors and social workers involved in the adoption racket. She told me that no one challenged her naming them because they knew they had done what she said.

In 2004 and again in 2009 Channel 9's *Sixty Minutes* featured the Hamilton-Byrne cult. Among the people interviewed were Sarah Moore and chief investigator on the case, Lex de Man. De

Man spoke of his anger about Hamilton-Byrne being let off with just a fine, calling her 'the most evil woman I have ever known'. The former investigator confirmed that a range of people from at least one major Melbourne hospital had been involved in the illegal adoptions. He added that he did not believe an independent investigation was ever held into how these professionals were able to conduct such a sophisticated adoption racket.

One government officer I interviewed for *Mothers in ARMS*, who insisted on remaining anonymous, said that more than one social worker was implicated in the scam but nothing happened to them because it was believed they were 'simply gullible'. 'After all,' the source said, 'there could be no other possible reason for their behaviour.' The idea that social workers could commit a crime was incomprehensible. And so it appeared to have been dismissed as simply poor judgement on the part of some well-meaning, albeit naïve, public servants.

If any Victoria Health Services Commissioner investigation was undertaken it was never reported, and neither was any internal government investigation. One newspaper stated that Community Services Victoria had rejected a call for an independent inquiry and police had reviewed adoption files held by the Department and found no need for further investigation. The police were, however, continuing to examine the files held by other former adoption agencies. When I asked Community Services Victoria recently if it ever investigated these illegal adoptions, it said it was a matter for the police and not Community Services. The Department had, however, reviewed its adoption regulations making it unlikely the same thing could happen again.

While researching this issue for *Mothers in ARMS*, I contacted Lex de Man for additional comments on the case. I put to him that one newspaper reported the police investigation came to a halt because adoption records went missing and there was not enough evidence to prosecute anyone other than the lawyer and a couple of pension fraudsters. De Man replied that the statement was not true. And with an air of frustrating but admirable professionalism, he refused to say more. He did indicate, however, that one day he would like to write a book on the Hamilton-Byrne cult, and if he does there will undoubtedly be many standing in line to read it.

In 2013 the Victorian Government changed its legislation, at last allowing mothers and fathers the right to apply for identifying information about their children. Whether or not more mothers will find their babies were given to Hamilton-Byrne, or simply disappeared without trace, remains to be seen.

What is clear is the fact that the Hamilton-Byrne adoptions were illegal and yet there seems have been little attention paid to bringing to justice the people who provided the babies to the cult. Even the journalists who reported on the cult appeared to focus on Hamilton-Byrne and the children who were at Eildon. No one seemed to explore the criminal practice of illegally taking newborn babies from vulnerable mothers, or ask what it might have meant to the young women who had been lied to by people who were supposed to be there to help them. And the fact that these unscrupulous professionals appear not to have been brought to account adds to the betrayal. It continues to give mothers and their children the impression that the crime was not serious enough to warrant the full force of the law being brought against the perpetrators, or the view that those who participated in it were naïve innocents rather than criminals who were complicit in a heinous crime.

ARMS came away from the Hamilton-Byrne cult experience wiser about what might lie in store for its mothers if laws were changed enabling them to find their children. Not only were adoptions illegal because women had not given a fully informed and free consent, but some of them were going to find that their babies had been brought up in homes of horror.

ARMS was even more determined to fight for the rights of its mothers but it also knew that it was going to need to provide professional counselling and support along the way, and who would be better to oversee that process than the women themselves.

12

A Dream Come True

BY THE END of 1987 I was in the throes of writing up my social work thesis – *Relinquishing Mothers: A Forgotten Group*. In particular I was looking at the laws, policies and social conditions that limited a mother's ability to be self-determining in South Australia. It was restricted to South Australia because each State had different legislation and all but Victoria were still in the process of reviewing their adoption Acts with the view to opening up secret records.

When looking through the legislation one day I noted a section in the Act I had never heard of before. It said that the Director-General, who became the interim guardian of the baby once a consent to adoption had been signed and the revocation period had passed, could place the baby with an adoptive family, or somewhere else, as deemed appropriate. On further exploration I realised it meant the child could be placed in an institution or in long-term foster care without ever being adopted, and these alternative arrangements could be made without the mother's consent or knowledge. But that was not what was written on the consent form. It only stated that the mother was giving a consent to 'adoption'. It concerned me particularly because, when I signed the consent form, no one told me that my baby might not be adopted. On the contrary, I was being told to give her up so that she would be adopted! The possibility that she might spend her life in a foster home or, worse still, an institution was simply never mentioned. And needless to say, it was never stated that if she was not adopted I might never be told.

I asked other mothers if they knew about the broader powers that could be invoked once a consent to adoption had been taken. The answer was a unanimous no.

'But we only gave consent to adoption,' they said, one after another. 'Surely, if our children weren't going to be adopted the Department would have had to let us know so we could take them home? How could they not tell us? After all they were the ones saying we had to give our babies up in the first place.' They were very fair questions.

I contacted Adoption Services to ask if what I was thinking was correct and I was advised that the *Adoption of Children Act 1967* did have a section in it that allowed the Director-General to place children in alternative care if adoption seemed unlikely. I was assured that, in those cases, every attempt was made to find the mother to let her know. However, where that was not possible the Act allowed for the placement to occur without her knowledge or consent. No one could tell me how many of these cases had occurred and how many mothers had not been informed their babies were not adopted.

I asked a couple of the staff who had witnessed consents if they knew a consent to adoption could mean that a baby might not be adopted and that it could be placed in permanent alternative care without the mother's consent or knowledge. I was told that no one had considered a consent to adoption meant anything other than 'adoption' and so nothing other than that was mentioned to mothers. I had a couple of consent forms from the 1960s as well as a 1987 consent form and neither the latest adoption brochure nor the documents spoke about anything other than adoption.

On the strength of my own experience, combined with the fact that the consent form only stipulated 'adoption', and that witnesses were only telling mothers about adoption, ARMS wrote to the Department stating the belief there was an 'anomaly' in the form that needed to be rectified urgently. ARMS said that past adoption consent forms had been extremely misleading, arguably illegal, and that it appeared the current 1987 consent form was similar.

Adoption Services agreed the form was misleading and that it would be changed as soon as the new Adoption Act went through, expected to be the following year. The Department said it would change the adoption brochure immediately and that all mothers considering adoption in future would be told about the broader powers of a consent to adoption.

From that time on ARMS had no doubt that many thousands of consents were invalid because mothers did not give an informed consent. How could it be 'informed' when the form was wrong and witnesses were not saying anything because they did not know it themselves? I wrote a chapter on the subject in my thesis and periodically ARMS raised the issue to argue the illegality of many adoptions. No one really knew what to make of it. But no one said that ARMS was wrong either.

Whilst writing *Mothers in ARMS* I revisited the issue of the anomaly in the consent form and I sought forms from other States to see if they were similar to the one used in South Australia. They were, and none other than the Tasmanian consent form authorised anything except adoption. I spoke with mothers from all around Australia and none of them knew about the full meaning of the form. I also interviewed social workers and other witnesses to consents during the 1960s and 1970s, and I talked with professionals who had written extensively on mothers and their adoption experience. I wanted to know if anyone knew that a consent to adoption had broader powers than adoption and if they told girls about it when they were witnessing consents.

Professor Karen Healy, President of the Australian Association of Social Workers, said she had not heard of it and she believed that social workers would have relied on what was written on the consent form to accurately reflect the legislation. 'They would have been acting in good faith that the consent forms were correct,' she said.

Margaret McDonald had worked in adoption for thirty years and had written a book with fellow retired social worker Audrey Marshall titled *The Many Sided Triangle – Adoption in Australia*.

Margaret was less surprised by the implicit meaning of the consent form. She said she did know that adoption was not the only thing the consent authorised but she believed the mother would be contacted to consent to the baby becoming a ward of the State if adoption was not likely. She admitted, however, that not all mothers could be found and under those circumstances their consent was waived. She concluded that even though she did not tell the girls they must have known because the fuller meaning of giving 'consent to adoption' would have been written somewhere on the New South Wales consent form. It was not.

Professor Dorothy Scott, now of the Australian Centre of Child Protection, also acknowledged that as a young social worker she did not tell the small number of mothers from whom she took consents that their babies might not be adopted because she was not aware of it. The focus had always seemed to be on working with couples around adopting a baby and there was no social work training in the taking of consents.

At the end of my research I concluded that this issue was far more widespread than I had first thought when writing my thesis in 1987 and I wondered about the mothers who in more recent years had sought information about their babies only to discover they were never adopted. And then there were the vast majority of mothers who were bullied into consenting to adoption but never told that it might never happen and they might not be told. I put my research to one side and vowed that I would come back to this issue one day.

ARMS had been a goldmine for a budding social work student placement. I was allowed to facilitate the mothers' support groups, which, if the truth be known, actually ran themselves. The women were desperate to talk to one another and were so committed to coming to the meetings that there was not much for me to do except make sure that everyone got a chance to speak if they wished to. The bigger problem for me was that it was sometimes difficult to just be the social work student because as a mother myself I also wanted to talk about my baby, now almost nineteen, but I knew I had to confine myself to 'appropriate and purposeful self disclosure' as a social worker and not a mother. Of course I lapsed a lot of the time and, frankly, I was glad that my student days were coming to an end and I could return to being one of the gang.

I did some individual counselling but it was difficult because none of my social work books had taught this kind of grief and loss therapy. Not much was written on the subject and it was obviously different from the 'normal' kind of loss felt by parents grieving the death of a child. With adoption, the baby had gone but was probably – hopefully – still out there somewhere. These mothers' grief could never be resolved because they had no body to put to rest and no grave to visit. I could never get them past the questions: Is he still alive? Will I meet her? What will I say if we ever get a chance to talk to one another? I knew exactly what they meant because they were my questions too. I was never going to resolve my own grief until I knew what had happened to my daughter. As a counsellor the best I could do was to help the mothers understand their own experience more broadly; that they were not bad girls and that they were not guilty of abandoning their babies. And so I muddled along using bits and pieces of everything I had learned at university and hoping like mad that something was working.

I felt more competent in my role as a community educator and political activist during my placement. Valma was a zealot, making sure that politicians, government departments, and anyone who would listen knew about ARMS and the issues for its mothers. Consequently I got to know the political process and how to access politicians as a means of affecting change. I also read extensively and kept in touch with the other ARMS groups who, like South Australia, were buzzing with anticipation that their governments would change the laws to let mothers find their children. They were truly exciting days and there was optimism in the air. As a social work student I could not have asked for a better place to learn about the profession – and about myself.

By December 1987 I was in the middle of writing up my thesis and I was a little surprised to get a call from a social worker in

Adoption Services saying she needed to talk to me about something important. I knew the woman well and I thought it was curious that instead of her usual calm voice she sounded excited in a way I had not heard before.

'I have just spoken to your daughter, Meg,' she said. 'She wants to meet you.'

For some reason I tried to be 'professional' and I replied as though I had been expecting her call and that the news was not really a surprise. I imagine it was some strange need to stop myself from bursting into tears and screaming with joy – and relief. (Mothers' emotions were often subdued or ill fitting when it came to discussions about their lost children.) In any event it was a surprise and when I put the phone down I began to shake uncontrollably. She's found me, I thought. It was the thing I had dreamt about for as long as I could remember and against all odds it had actually happened. I could not believe how lucky I was.

My daughter turned nineteen on 1 November 1987 and she had put her name on the Adoption Contact Register on the off-chance that I might do the same. What she did not know was that I had been on it for years. I knew she could not look for me before she turned eighteen but I wanted to leave a letter for her in case something happened to me in the meantime. And when she turned eighteen and I knew she could register I contacted her birthfather through a mutual friend and asked if he wanted to put his name down too. The message came back that he had always felt terrible about what had happened and he wanted to meet his daughter if she wanted to know him. So when she registered both her birth parents were there waiting for her. Of the several thousand people who put their names down during the Contact Register's ten years of operation only 180 matches were made.

It was agreed that my daughter would meet me first and that she would see her birth father a short while later. I was happy with that plan because I had not seen my ex-boyfriend for nearly twenty years and I needed to come to terms with the possibility of meeting him again. And as my daughter had not expected to find even one of her birth parents on the Register, much less both of them, she was somewhat overwhelmed by the reality of it all.

The Contact Register had been a radical concept for its time and it was quite out of kilter with the existing secret adoption legislation. Consequently the Department played a significant role in overseeing the first meeting between consenting people and it generally occurred in an office in the Adoption Services Department. A social worker would do the initial introduction and, after a short while, if everyone seemed to be getting on reasonably well she would excuse herself and leave them to get on with the business of getting to know one another. I knew the social worker who was going to supervise our first meeting and I trusted her implicitly. She was gentle and kind, and extremely sensitive to the nuances of meetings as strange as these ones, and I knew she would not leave the room if she could see either my daughter or I needed her to stay.

I sat in the waiting room with my legs crossed at the ankles and my hands clasped together in my lap. I was trying to stay calm but there was a constant flutter in my chest reminding me that in the very next room was the baby who had wrapped her tiny fingers around mine all those years ago, and that now she wanted to meet me. The social worker opened the door and asked if I would like to come in. And there she stood, smiling and holding in her arms a huge bunch of purple everlasting flowers – the symbolism was profound.

We hugged and stared and talked, and after a few minutes the social worker discreetly excused herself. Her timing was impeccable. We chatted for a little while longer and then decided it was time to escape the confines of the Adoption Services office. We found a lovely restaurant on a lake and sat in the sunshine eating from a fish platter, talking and laughing like we had known one another all our lives.

I was fascinated by how much she looked like me. And when she got up I noticed how she walked with a slight bounce in her step, as if walking on the balls of her feet. I had seen that walk before. It was just like her birth father's walk and I was struck by the fact that adopted children, even though they may never have met their parents, inherit many more traits than just looks.

After a long lunch we went to my home and I introduced my daughter to my husband and her seven-year-old half sister. We looked at old photos and shared histories. And when she left we hugged and exchanged numbers. We knew that we meant it when we promised to call one another soon.

Nineteen years earlier, when I signed the consent form, I had hoped beyond hope that one day my daughter would come looking for me. And she had. I could not say it to her but I felt immensely proud of her. It was as if she were a small child who had got lost and had found her way back home. I knew it was an idiotic thought but I felt it all the same. That night I rang Valma and I cried like a baby. I was so glad to have her, and ARMS. I did not have to say a word. She knew I needed to cry for all the years I had not known my daughter, with relief that she had survived her childhood, and with joy that she wanted to know me.

I passed my final year of social work and my two daughters, my husband and my mother attended my graduation ceremony. We celebrated my daughter's twenty-first birthday with her parents and not too many years after that we all attended her wedding. She and her husband now have a glorious daughter and we have known the family for over twenty-six years.

13

Ethical Dilemmas

IT HAD BEEN A HEADY YEAR for ARMS. It had found its feet as a support organisation and as a political voice with some credibility, and by 1987 its staff were regarded as experts in the experiences of mothers. After Adoption Services released its review findings – and had excluded mothers from its recommendations – ARMS, being more than a little miffed, decided to conduct its own phone survey to see what women thought about the perceived snub.

More than a hundred people responded, and although they were overwhelmingly in favour of adoptees being given the right to receive identifying information they were worried about being reliant on their children to make the first move. How would they be able to make contact if they did not know they were adopted? What if they had believed the lies about adoption and did not think their mothers would want to know them? Mothers were also angry about having been left out of the recommendations. What did that say about them? Was it that they could not be trusted to behave properly if they had identifying information about their children? Were they still seen as not deserving any rights because they had given up their babies for adoption? They felt like they were being judged and punished all over again.

There was another niggling concern. It was that small group of mothers who were ringing up to say they were terrified about their children getting identifying information about them. They had not told their husbands or their families. They had never spoken about the secret shame and they were afraid they would be abandoned by their families all over again if the truth came out. They did not want ARMS to fight for their rights to get identifying information. They wanted ARMS to protect them from their children having it.

It was the group ARMS had never wanted to think about. If these mothers were acknowledged, then ARMS had to accept that some women needed a veto to stop their children from knowing who they were. It flew in the face of the view that ARMS had been promoting from the very beginning; that mothers wanted to know their children and that they were all prepared for the consequences of a reunion.

And there was another group ARMS did not want to dwell on – fathers. Mothers, in the main, were not very sympathetic to the needs of the men who had left them in the lurch, and they did not necessarily believe they were interested in seeing their children anyway. Even some mothers who had married the fathers were not altogether happy with their husbands having too much say about adoption and it may have been a strategy to punish them for the part they played in their babies being given up. Overall, it was seen as a women's issue. Nevertheless, men were significantly disadvantaged in all areas of adoption. Mothers were often discouraged from naming the fathers on the original birth certificate, the argument being that if they were registered they could contest the adoption. For many mothers this was hardly a realistic likelihood, but they complied anyway and many times the certificate recorded 'father – unknown'. By not being registered fathers had no right to stop identifying information being released about them, and they had no right to apply for it without the written permission of the mother. They were totally at the behest of mothers who were sometimes still angry and reluctant to let them meet their children, or to keep their names a secret. It was a powerless and unenviable position to be in, but ARMS, not wanting to antagonise its mothers, resolved that it did not have to be an advocate for fathers' rights. It was, after all, a service for mothers. It was written into its constitution. The only time it had to fight for fathers was if it impacted upon the mother. And so ARMS put the issue to one side, aware that fathers' lack of rights was wrong, but that it was unable to think of a way of addressing the problem without angering and upsetting the women it represented.

ARMS did eventually allow fathers to come to support groups but in the words of one father: 'Going to a meeting was like being in a Woody Allen movie. Everyone just sat around talking about their feelings. I wanted to be outside doing something with a piece of wood.' ARMS knew it would never be able to effectively work with fathers and sadly it would be another twenty years before any serious firsthand account of being a birth father would be written and the rights and needs of the men in adoption would be recognised as an issue.

Undeterred by its ethical dilemmas, ARMS made its first submission for substantial funding in late 1987. It asked the government for the tidy sum of $110,732.35 for a coordinator, administrator, social worker and typist. It did not get it but it was a brave request and ARMS never stopped asking for the moon. It firmly believed that one day someone in the Funding Unit would pick up the latest submission and see that this was a bunch of women who were serious about their cause and that they were not going away.

Whilst it debated the way it could fairly represent all mothers, ARMS also made a submission to the Director-General for Community Welfare to make hospital records accessible to mothers' doctors when the mothers had subsequent children. It was met with a few raised eyebrows and some peculiar responses.

Under the secrecy legislation most public hospitals had a system wherein the baby-for-adoption and the mother's records were separate files with separate UR numbers. They could not be linked with one another without verification from Adoption Services. And when a mother had a subsequent baby her doctor did not have access to any information about the first child's medical history at birth – and because of the secrecy in adoption neither did the mother. This was a frustration for mothers and paediatricians where a subsequent child had a medical problem that might have been anticipated if only they had known about the first baby's health at birth. But by the time the doctor made an application to see the file and it had gone to medical records, and then to Adoption Services for the information to link the two files, some weeks had passed and the medical crisis had either been averted, or dealt with in the absence of information about the first baby.

Getting anyone to acknowledge this was an issue was itself a problem. No one except the mothers and a handful of paediatricians seemed to realise who ARMS was talking about.

'The information about the baby is not relevant,' ARMS was told by more than one doctor, 'because that baby is not biologically the same as the mother. She's an "adoptive" mother, after all.' ARMS replied that it was not talking about adoptive mothers. It was talking about the biological mother of the baby and that the information about the first child was important when the mother had subsequent children. Again, the response was curious.

'But those girls don't have any more children,' ARMS was told. And when one doctor was assured that most mothers did have more children she replied, 'Well, I have never seen one because I would know one if I saw one.' The doctor did not elaborate on how she would 'know one' but ARMS presumed she must have thought they had a tattoo on their foreheads saying 'relinquishing mother', or some such thing.

Fortunately enough paediatricians came on board to show that there genuinely was an issue and the government agreed to cross-reference mothers' and babies' records more appropriately so that hospitals could access medical information promptly.

As 1987 came to a close ARMS learned that Rosemary Wighton's draft Adoption Bill had been referred to an All-Party Select Committee for further public consultation and consideration. Interested parties were being asked to make submissions to the Committee, either in writing or in person. The main issue, as ARMS saw it, concerned whether or not records should be opened retrospectively and, if they should, who could apply for identifying information. Adoption Services had made its views clear, and Victoria had already grappled with this issue and erred on the side of caution by only giving rights to adoptees.

ARMS Victoria had been devastated by its State's decision to leave mothers out of the new Adoption Act. The group had fought long and hard for them to be included in the Bill and for a time it looked as though it was going to be successful. At the eleventh hour, however, the Victorian Government bowed to pressure from a strong adoptive parents lobby group and mothers were virtually cut out of the legislation. ARMS Victoria warned South Australia to be careful, telling its sister group that when its turn came maybe it should push for adoptee rights first rather than agitating for mothers at the same time and risk ending up with nothing at all.

ARMS in South Australia decided to ignore the well intentioned advice. 'We are an organisation for relinquishing mothers,' Valma said defiantly. 'If we don't fight for the rights of mothers now what are we here for?'

And of course she was right. But it was risky business. No other country in the English-speaking world with similar adoption legislation had given mothers the right to apply for identifying information about their children. And Rosemary Wighton's Bill had been referred to a Select Committee for further deliberation, so clearly nothing had been decided.

Nevertheless, ARMS believed there was a different mood in South Australia. The State had had several progressive governments in recent years and there was strong bi-partisanship between Labor, Liberal and the Australian Democrats when it came to social justice issues. South Australia was the first State in Australia, and one of the first places in the world, to give women the vote. With those credentials, ARMS believed that if radical legislation was going to get up anywhere, South Australia would be the place to make it happen. And so, with fingers crossed tightly, the ARMS Management Committee voted unanimously to push for mothers and fathers to be given the same access to identifying information as adopted adults.

It was not going to be easy sailing and the Select Committee would raise at least one of those sticky issues ARMS had not wanted to think about. But if ARMS succeeded in convincing them that mothers should be included in the new Bill it would make history not only in this country, but around the world.

14

The Big Debate

ARMS HAD SPENT MONTHS poring over the proposed Bill so it could fairly represent all parties when it made its submission to the Select Committee early in 1988. Of course, by *all parties* it really only meant mothers and those adopted. Fathers were not given much thought and ARMS knew it could never represent adoptive parents, apart from Lila's group who were in favour of giving mothers rights.

ARMS primary objective, barring certain exceptional circumstances, was to give mothers, and adoptees over the age of eighteen, the original birth certificate as well as identifying information so they could make contact with one another. If one party did not want the other party to have identifying information it would be withheld for a period of six months while counselling was offered, and at the end of that time it would be given out unless a good reason could be provided for not releasing it. If a good reason was found, the applicant, regardless of who it was, would not receive any identifying information, including the original birth certificate.

ARMS knew there were large numbers of adoptive parents who were totally opposed to opening adoption records. They had received their babies with the promise of permanent secrecy and the knowledge that the mother would never be able to come back into the child's life. Although the public view had been that mothers had abandoned their babies and had no interest in seeing them again, the legislation ensured that they could not do so – just in case. It was understandable that, having been assured the mother could never find her child, adoptive parents were worried about the prospect of records being opened and identifying information being released.

Heated debates raged and some adoptees were also angry about information being given to mothers who, they believed, had rejected them at birth. Others professed not to want to know their mothers because they did not want to hurt their adoptive parents. One public figure, an adoptive parent, was very vocal, claiming that those adopted had no interest in finding their biological parents and it was simply propaganda put about by Adoption Services because it had no work to do since the dramatic decline in adoptions over recent years. Unbeknownst to the angry parent, it was not a view shared by all of the person's children.

The Select Committee was to be chaired by Dr John Cornwall, who was now the Minister for Community Welfare, and made up of representatives from all the parties, including the newly formed Australian Democrats (whose motto was 'We're here to keep the bastards honest') and a senior person from the Adoption Services Department.

Valma and I planned that we would talk primarily to ARMS's submission and that another mother would speak about her personal experience of adoption. We calculated that if we had to do both jobs ourselves the Committee would likely be distracted from our submission in favour of hearing stories about our personal experiences. (Mothers' relinquishments and reunions with their children were a fascination to most people, and politicians were no different from anyone else.) We knew we were at the hearing representing ARMS and it was not the time or place to be pouring out our own life stories. Besides, there was one particular recommendation that was going to need some serious arguing if ARMS was going to get support for it across parties.

Valma decided that if ARMS was going to prove that mothers could have contact with their children without upsetting the equilibrium of the 'family', the mother who was going to speak to the Committee would have been reunited with her child and would then be able to speak authentically about contact. She would show that mothers, their children and the adoptive families could all meet and have positive relationships with one another. She would be fair-minded, intelligent and articulate and she would show the politicians that mothers could be trusted not to steal their children away from the adoptive families. Valma knew just the woman.

Veronica had a calm demeanour, and a wisdom and honesty about her experience that made you know she was not trying to pull the wool over your eyes. She had met her son some years earlier in Victoria and their contact was going extremely well, including her relationship with the adoptive parents. She was the best person to demonstrate that mothers were normal rational human beings who were responsible and could be sensitive to the situation when they met their children. Fortunately Veronica agreed.

The hearings were held in Parliament House and the room where people were to make their submissions was dark and typically old-English in its fixtures and fittings. Around the perimeter of the room, with just enough space to allow people to sit, were a series of long scratched mahogany tables joined together to form a large rectangle with an open centre. The chairperson sat at the top end of the rectangle with a scribe to his left, and down each side sat the politicians as well as a social worker from Adoption Services. Witnesses came in from the other end of the room and it was a formidable task to walk into the echoey chamber under the watchful gaze of the Committee members. To them it was probably just another day at the office and the mothers were somewhat of a curiosity. To the ARMS representatives, as complete novices, it was daunting.

Valma and I sat down with a bevy of folders, files and pens, desperately trying to look professional and fooling absolutely no one. Veronica on the other hand, looked as cool, calm and collected as she always did. We knew that she was not going to be a problem at the Hearing but if we did not calm down, we were!

Dr Cornwall introduced the Committee members individually and then asked if each of us would talk briefly about ourselves.

Valma said she was chair of ARMS, a relinquishing mother and a student doing her BA at university. I said that I had just finished my final year social work placement at ARMS and expected to have my degree shortly. I was also a relinquishing mother. Veronica said she had no qualifications and she was a relinquishing mother and had met her son several years ago. We all remarked later that it was one of the proudest moments of our lives to be standing in Parliament House and declaring that we were mothers. How we had changed.

ARMS first recommendation was that the definition of consent must be clear on consent forms in any new adoption legislation. We highlighted that women had signed forms giving consent to adoption only. They had not been told that they were actually consenting to guardianship if adoption did not take place. One of the Committee members asked if there had been examples of mothers giving consent to adoption where it did not occur and I cited a case in New South Wales where a mother had learned many years after giving consent that her son had never been adopted and had died at the age of twelve in an institution. She told ARMS that if she had known her little boy was going to spend his entire life in an institution she would have done all she could to make his short life as happy as possible.

The issue of guardianship as an alternative to adoption was also raised because ARMS noted that the Bill proposed that, where possible, Aboriginal children should be placed under the guardianship of extended families instead of being placed for adoption. ARMS wondered why adoption could not be the exception rather than the rule with all children, regardless of race, but the argument fell flat because we did not know enough about the differences between adoption and guardianship to argue the issue cogently. It was a matter ARMS would return to in later years, when it finally declared it was opposed to adoption in any form. But that would be later.

Next up was the issue of who should be eligible to adopt. ARMS put its view forward that a person's eligibility to apply to adopt a child should not be based on gender or marital status. It believed that children should be placed with families or individuals who would love and care for them, and experience had shown that that did not equate with having to be heterosexual and married. ARMS view was noted and not debated.

Most ARMS members signed their consents to adoption only a week or so after the baby's birth. ARMS argued to the Committee that most women were still traumatised from the delivery and from being deprived of their babies, and that making them give consent so soon after such a traumatic event was inappropriate. ARMS believed that in future women should not give consent until at least fourteen days after the birth. The Committee was reminded that the original intent of the new adoption Act was that consent could be given as early as five days after the birth, but only under special circumstances. ARMS said that this had been left out of the draft Bill. Instead it read that the court only had to be satisfied that the mother was in a rational state of mind if she gave consent after five days and before fourteen days from the delivery date. ARMS wanted to make sure that fourteen days was the accepted appropriate amount of time, and any less could only be done if fully justified.

The next submission concerned the original birth certificates. ARMS had always believed that adopted adults should be allowed to have their original birth certificates naming their parent(s). But ARMS also wanted mothers to have a copy of the original birth certificate, for a different reason. It was the document never given to them when their children were born, and when the adoption was formalised the original birth certificate was cancelled, never to see the light of day again. ARMS argued that the certificate should never have been kept from mothers in the first place because it contained their names as the true parent of the child and it recorded the names they had given their babies. ARMS said the documents did not identify the adopted person's new name and that as an act of restitution the government should make these certificates available to mothers now.

Now the submission became challenging. ARMS had always put to the back of its mind the mothers who, for whatever reason, did not want identifying information released to anyone. They may have had different views from ARMS, but they were still mothers and they needed representation.

Valma and I began our argument by saying that mothers, like adopted adults, should be allowed to apply for identifying information. ARMS could see no reason why the law should not be equitable in this regard. Adopted people would be allowed to look for their mothers and mothers should also be able to look for their now adult children. It was fairly straightforward, or so we thought!

Then, to accommodate the mothers who did not want information released (and that included adopted people who felt the same way), ARMS suggested information be withheld for a period of six months while the person refusing to allow disclosure had counselling.

The Committee immediately picked up on the word 'counselling' and wanted to know if it actually meant that the person had to enter into some kind of therapy. I tried to explain that it was more like an interview than therapeutic counselling and that it was designed to help the person explore their concerns about information being released. One politician asked if the purpose of the counselling might be to coerce the person into letting the other party have the information. I said it was simply a mechanism for allowing the person to discuss their fears and if at the end of the interview they still thought it would be too traumatic for the information to be given out, then it would not be passed on – not even the original birth certificate to the adoptee. There was a collective gasp in the room and the politicians shuffled papers, and their feet.

All the political parties, and Adoption Services, had been supportive of adopted people's belief that they had a fundamental right to have their original birth certificate, and the Committee was ready to include it in the new Adoption Act. ARMS had, in principle, believed the same thing. Its members were generally more than happy for their children to have the document that could identify who they were. After all, more than anything ARMS mothers wanted to meet their children and they believed their children should be entitled to have their birth certificates just like everyone else in society. But ARMS also had to think about the women who were simply terrified of the thought of identifying information being released, and who had no public voice to speak on their behalf.

And so, even though ARMS had never really wanted a veto on information being given out, it found itself supporting the Committee's recommendation that one be included.

The Committee asked if ARMS would agree to the birth certificate being given to the adopted adult if the person signed a legal document saying they would not make contact with the mother. But ARMS could not agree. It felt it would be asking too much of adoptees to give them the information and then say they were not allowed to approach the person in any way. And if they did breach the condition of no contact how could anyone with a conscience impose a financial or other kind of penalty on them?

And so, with ARMS permission to adjust the submission if required, Valma and I stumbled through negotiations that significantly watered down what we had really wanted. ARMS had never wanted a veto but it knew it could not support identifying information being given out if the mother or adoptee genuinely did not want it disclosed. ARMS also worried that if it did not accept a veto mothers would not be given equal rights to identifying information.

Then, clearly not comfortable with our new position, Valma found herself talking about her own situation where she had identifying information about her daughter but had always respected her privacy and had never approached her. It was flying directly in the face of our argument that one could not expect people not to breach their obligation to stay away from the other party if they had their name and knew their whereabouts. To make matters worse I followed on from Valma and said that if the government really insisted on it, we would agree to adoptees having their original birth certificates. Talk about not being committed to our own position!

The whole thing was a complete shemozzle and amid looks of

sheer confusion on the faces of the politicians Dr Cornwall perceptively said that it seemed we were trying to accommodate a very wide spectrum of opinion. He said it appeared we were trying to help women who did not want contact and did not want any information to be given to their children but we also wanted to represent mothers who were desperately keen to find their children and who believed their children should have their original birth certificates. He was right, and it was clear that we were all over the place. The chairman smiled knowingly and added that he thought we were a bit like the AMA, trying to look after GPs and the full spectrum of specialists at the very same time. Valma replied by saying that women were carers and were used to looking after everybody. Dr Cornwall answered, 'But it presents you with a very difficult task.'

Valma responded, 'It does, but we try to be fair.'

And therein lay the dilemma. It was simply impossible to be fair to everyone. We concluded our submission feeling utterly drained but knowing we had done our best.

The chairman then turned to Veronica and asked if she would be kind enough to tell the Committee a little bit about how she met her son and what it was like for them both now. In her wonderfully soothing way she proceeded to captivate the entire room with the story of how she had relinquished in Victoria and had been trying to find her boy for a number of years before the laws changed in that State in 1984. After counselling and the sharing of non-identifying information between the two families, Veronica met her son and his parents. He was twenty-two years old.

'What does your son call you?' one of the politicians asked.

'Mum,' Veronica said easily.

'And how about you, Ms Hale?' someone else asked.

'My daughter calls me Meg,' I answered.

It was an often-asked question and one that always seemed to be of significant interest to the person making the enquiry. Mothers were never sure which was the preferred answer. In this situation we were lucky because there was one of each and we hoped our answers satisfied the Committee overall.

The Committee went on to ask about our relationships with our children and if we felt like we were their mothers. Dr Cornwall said he could see Veronica talked very naturally about her son and his parents and it was clear she saw herself as his mother and that the adoptive parents were his parents. She replied that he had a South Australian mother and a Victorian mother. This, for him, was very good. For her it was 'simply excellent'. Everyone smiled and nodded happily. Then they asked me.

I cringe when I remember what I said to the entire Committee and which, to this day, is recorded in Hansard for anyone to read. Instead of giving an illustration similar to Veronica's I chose to say something quite different. I told them that I was more like a friend to my daughter than a parent. And I should have stopped there, but I did not. I added that whereas I might get drunk with my friends, I would not get drunk with my daughter because there were limits on what I would do with her because I was her mother. As the words came out of my mouth I knew they were horrendously inappropriate. As well as having to dress smartly, mothers – and certainly ARMS management committee members – could not be seen to have vices, and I had just declared to the entire Select Committee that I was not averse to getting sloshed with my pals. The only saving grace was that I added that I would not be taking my daughter out on the town any time soon!

We made a few other recommendations and our evidence concluded with some wise words from the chairperson about how we were all sitting here playing God and it was important that any future legislation had a minimum of intrusion and interference and that it contained a lot of commonsense. We all nodded approvingly and withdrew.

The post mortem of the day's events was mixed. We recognised we had changed tack about twenty times during the hearing and we hoped no one noticed! I reminded Valma we were supposed to be saying we did not think people could be expected to have identifying information and not act on it, and that she had completely undone our own argument when she said she knew where her daughter was and that she had never breached her wishes not to be contacted (something she might wish she had never said as events unfolded in the months to come). In turn, she reminded me that I had been saying 'absolutely no' to adoptees being given their birth certificates and then in the next breath I had said that if the government really wanted to include it in the Act we would not object. Then there was the bit where I told them I would get drunk with my friends but not with my daughter ... because, after all, I was her mother. Then the three of us started to laugh.

We finished our review by deciding it had not been a complete debacle and that we had made some salient points. We congratulated one another on how well we had handled the situation given how nervous we had all felt. None of us had been inside Parliament House before, much less tried to unravel a piece of legislation that was so close to our hearts. And then we had to repack it so that it was not only fair to ARMS mothers but it also represented those silent women out there who had no one to speak for them.

We hugged as we said goodbye, knowing that what we had asked for had been refused to Victoria and was not being seriously considered elsewhere. If we succeeded it would make Australian history. We had asked our government to give us the same rights as our children and allow mothers to apply for identifying information so they could make contact with their lost families. All we had to do now was wait.

15

Bitter Surrender

ANN SHARLEY MIGHT HAVE FINISHED her social work placement but she had not stopped thinking about ARMS and its mothers. An idea had been rolling around in her head for some time – an idea about making a film showing the journey mothers went on from the time they became pregnant to the pain they experienced by losing their babies through adoption. She had no background in filmmaking, but that was not about to stop her.

After many film grant refusals Ann knew she had to establish some credibility with the documentary film industry before anyone was going to take her seriously as a filmmaker. She had no background in writing, editing or producing, and she had never set foot in a film school, so she decided to find out more by going to a seminar on the topic. Once there, she hoped she would learn something about the art of documentary filmmaking and, more importantly, find out who she would need to help her and where to find them.

The South Australian Media Resource Centre was a place where budding filmmakers gathered and shared resources and ideas. Ann and a friend who was also interested in the project decided to go along to see if anyone there might want to help make a documentary on adoption – with a twist. It would be from the mother's perspective.

Francesca da Rimini, a pint-sized dynamo in her twenties who knew a lot about filmmaking and had plenty of enthusiasm and talent, put her hand up immediately. She had some experience with

Super-8 filmmaking but was a complete novice in the area of 16 mm documentary films. But she liked the way the project was being presented and thought it might be fun to give the women a hand in getting it up and running. Francesca had no idea that people would leave along the way and that she would end up co-producing the film with Ann – and that it would take them five years to complete.

Initially Ann and Francesca had thought about making a documentary-drama film, using an actor to tell one woman's story from pregnancy through relinquishment and into the years following the adoption. But after several attempts at writing the script, they decided that nothing could replace the raw power of the unmediated voices of women who had experienced it themselves.

With their new outline now clear the two filmmakers approached the Australian Film Commission and were told that the project would only be funded if they used a professional director who had a good track record. When they came back to the Commission with the names of Louise Hubbard as director, Erica Addis as cinematographer, and Catherine Murphy as editor they were granted enough money to get the film off the ground. They were elated. And once the bank account looked a bit healthier they were able to add a fine film crew to the list of professionals working on the project.

Harrison and I joined the team as general helpers. Ann, Francesca and Harrison then met with the ARMS management committee to ask if they knew women who would be willing to take part in a documentary film on adoption. The filmmakers wanted mothers of different ages and experiences so the stories would be diverse and without bias towards a particular point of view. It was not an easy request. Mothers were coming out one by one and telling an abbreviated version of their stories in magazines and newspapers, but that was not the same as baring one's soul in a documentary designed to be shown far and wide. And it was hard to find an ARMS woman who had placed a baby for adoption recently. Since the early 1970s when mothers were granted the financial means to support their children and were no longer being forced to give them up due to poverty, adoptions in South Australia had dropped from around 800 to less than ten a year. And finding a mother from within the ARMS group who believed her decision to give her child up to adoption was voluntary, and right, was not easy either.

After some searching, the filmmakers found a brave young mother who had only relinquished three years earlier and felt she had made the right decision. Ann and Francesca also located a woman who had given her child up when he was three years old. Hers was a very different story. ARMS came up with some names as well; Valma and Veronica among them. Valma had lost her child in the 1950s after being sent interstate to a home for unmarried mothers. Veronica's son had been adopted in the 1960s and as they had been reunited she would be able to talk about what it was like to meet one's child, a stranger, after so many years.

The four women were perfect, providing a good cross-section of experiences and beliefs about adoption. They were also able to talk with passion without falling apart on camera. No one had any objection to the mothers crying – that would be the most natural thing to expect – but the film needed to tell a big story in a brief time and the filmmakers needed women who could show emotion but not allow it to overwhelm them to the point where they could not tell their stories.

Marie Meggitt, who was now chairperson of ARMS in Victoria, narrated the film and gave an overview of the social and political reasons that added to mothers' experiences of adoption. Some of the ARMS Victoria mothers also featured in the film while picketing in the streets of downtown Melbourne. They looked impressive. It was a very fine cast.

The film opened with some grainy Super 8 colour footage of well-dressed 1950s mothers in their hats and gloves showing off their newborn babies to the camera and admiring onlookers. Australian singer Jeannie Lewis sang the bluesy and potent song 'Motherless Child' during the introduction. No other piece of music could have been more apt.

Chris, the mother of the three-year-old, was the first to tell her story. At first it seemed a senseless and shocking act and one wondered how a woman could keep her child for three years and then give him up. But when she talked about how she had put motherhood on a pedestal and that she believed her son was suffering because he was in child care all the time so she could work two jobs to make ends meet, you got a very different view about her decision to give him up. And when she said that she realised she could not go through with it and that she tried to get him back you knew there was a lot more to this story than at first glance. The mother held back tears as she described how she drove all night to get to the adoption home in time to get him back before the revocation period expired. She banged on the agency door, calling out to them to let her have her son, and before it was slammed in her face someone angrily told her she was too late. Her time had elapsed at midday the day before. Her son was never returned to her.

Valma asked for her interview to be done in one of the common rooms at Flinders University where she was studying for an Arts Degree. She had decided to be filmed on campus because she thought she had a greater chance of keeping her emotions in check there, rather than if she were sitting in a cosy armchair in her own living room. And she was probably right. Generally Valma had a strong assertive manner – she needed it for the work she was doing – but when she talked about her own experience she knew she could become easily flustered and anxious. It was the legacy of how cruelly she had been treated during her pregnancy and afterwards. She knew that in a slightly less comfortable setting she would be able to tell her story with feeling but her surroundings would help her not get so caught up in the past that she lost herself completely.

In the interview her voice was childlike at times and you could imagine her as the young woman being scolded by her mother and then handed over to the nuns to be hidden away for the term of the pregnancy. At one point, when she talked about the moment her baby was taken from her, she looked upwards and the camera caught a glimpse of someone reliving a moment of utter despair. One of the most poignant parts of the interview, and the film, was when Valma said that after her baby had been taken from her a nun patted her on the back and told her that she would get over this and one day she would feel normal again. Trying to hold back tears Valma said, 'I was never to know what *normal* felt like after that.'

The youngest of the mothers appeared in the film next. Josie's baby had only been relinquished three years before. She had grown up in a single parent family and had watched her father struggle to raise his children on his own. She wanted far more than that for her son and she had given him up so he could have a better life than she thought she could give him. Early in the interview Josie described the feeling of loss as a gaping hole that was getting smaller as time went on. Later she said it was 'like a seeping wound that won't heal, as much as you want it to'. She went on to say that whereas death was final, with adoption the mother went on forever asking: 'Where are you? What's happening?' A person watching the interview might be left with mixed feelings about whether things were getting better for her or if she just needed to believe they were. Either way, you were left hoping that Josie was going to be one of those mothers who would feel all right about giving up her baby in years to come.

Veronica was filmed next and her easygoing manner came across particularly well. She had a hypnotic voice that made your skin tingle, and her garden formed a natural backdrop to the interview giving her words a calm and serene quality. She told how she felt suicidal after the births of each of her subsequent children but when she had counselling for her depression she never told any of the therapists about her first child. It was only when she began to look for her son that she started talking about her experience, first to Community Services Victoria and then at the Department's recommendation to a therapist in South Australia where she now lived. In the documentary Veronica talked about how she had called her baby Mark and it was difficult getting used to calling him Nicholas when she met him again as an adult.

'After a while I realised that Mark was all the pain and Nicholas is all the joy,' she said. 'Now I think of Nicholas as the person he really is.'

Marie Meggitt, who provided the voice-over for the film, had stood on the steps of Victoria's Parliament House in the early 1980s championing the rights of mothers and their children, and her inclusion in *Bitter Surrender* was no accident. She told how society was geared up to believe that there were two types of mothers. Deserving mothers were those women who were married, and single women were undeserving of their children because of their lack of marital status. She said that young mothers were swept along by the wave of opinion.

'Their powerlessness was incredibly frightening,' she said, talking about their, and her own, experience.

Some Victorian news footage was also spliced into the film and it showed Marie with a group of ARMS Victoria mothers holding up placards and handing out leaflets in the inner city. Victoria's laws had changed in 1984 but there was up to an eleven-year wait for adoptees to receive identifying information, or for the Department to make a decision about whether or not it would approach an adopted adult on behalf of a mother. One placard read: 'My mother died while I waited.' Other boards alluded to the Hamilton-Byrne cult (known locally as 'The Family') and in bold red print one read 'Malpractice, Adoption – The Family'. Another questioned the wording on the consent form and the fact that adoption did not necessarily mean only adoption. 'Is my child a state ward now?' one angry mother wrote.

The footage of the Victorian protests was powerful and so were the newspaper cuttings with headings like 'Motherless babies', 'Bastard children', 'Unwanted infants', and articles depicting surrogacy as the latest thing if you wanted a baby and adoption was either not available or it was just not your cup of tea.

'Our community has not even begun to think about the implications of surrogacy,' Marie argued. 'Or that in the context of our material society we are willing to see children as yet one more commodity to be dealt with.' They were powerful and prophetic words.

The documentary ran for nearly thirty minutes and ended with Marie summing up adoption. In her beautifully mellow voice she said, 'Mothers had been told they had nothing to offer their children, but what they had come to understand was that while they might not have a lot to give they do have a capacity to love. And children are best loved by many, not exclusively by a few.'

She concluded by saying, 'The hallmark of adoption is about ownership. It is about what is good enough for one woman is not good enough for another. It's about birth being right in some circumstances and wrong in others.'

And then she paused, and with an almost wistful sound in her voice she finished by saying, 'It's a very strange thing really.'

Bitter Surrender was launched on 30 March 1989 at Greater Union Cinema in Adelaide, and the filmmakers and some ARMS members shared a few words with the audience before the documentary was shown. In the theatre were mothers, fathers, family members, adopted people, adoptive parents, public servants and the people who had worked on the film tirelessly for five years.

Bitter Surrender was launched Australia-wide and was nominated for an ATOM (Australian Teachers of Media) Award. For many years it was used as a teaching tool in universities and colleges teaching social work and counselling, and it remains one of the most significant achievements ARMS has ever been associated with.

16

Only Human After All

IN NOVEMBER 1988 Valma and I flew to Melbourne to attend the national ARMS conference and then the International Adoption Conference, which was on immediately afterward. Valma's daughter was born in Victoria and we were particularly interested in how the law changes giving adopted adults identifying information were working in that State. We were told that processing applications, whilst improving, remained painfully slow and the waiting list was still several years long. It was a sorry state of affairs and people had died while they waited for information about their loved ones.

Valma had already asked the adoption agency about her daughter and had been told that the young woman did not want any identifying information given out. It was a cruel blow to Valma who had spent years helping other mothers and watching them establish relationships with their children. What the agency did not realise, however, was the fact that it had inadvertently passed on an interesting snippet of information. Scrawled on the back of a document sent to Valma were some indecipherable handwritten words. It was only when the page was put up to a mirror that it became clear that this was information that could help to identify her daughter.

Any typist from the baby boomer generation would remember the frustration of unwittingly putting carbon paper back to front in between two sheets of paper for typing, and only finding out when the typing was finished that the copy page was blank and the words were written in reverse on the back of the original work. It appeared that an adoptions worker had written a name on a piece of paper, unaware than underneath it was the letter to Valma and beneath that was a piece of carbon paper wrong side up. Valma had been holding onto this name for some time and it was now beginning to get the better of her.

Even when identifying information for mothers was still a thing of the future women had learned to be extremely creative about finding the whereabouts of their children. Now and then they would come into ARMS with the person's name and ask, 'What do I do now?' ARMS had a fairly conservative view about what to do next. There was no law saying a mother could not approach the adopted person directly, but ARMS knew there was a sensitive way to handle matters. The idea of turning up on the adopted person's doorstep was severely frowned upon, as it was for an adoptee to knock on the mother's door out of the blue. It was generally thought that a letter was the most appropriate first outreach, and that it might be best for an intermediary to handle the delicate initial contact.

Adoption Services had also long been of the view that a third party, preferably the Department, should act as an intermediary. Eventually it came to realise that agencies like ARMS and Jigsaw were equally competent at facilitating contacts and people were referred to the support groups on the understanding that the mother or adopted person would be encouraged to use a third person, and that over-zealous individuals would be dissuaded from arriving, unannounced, on the other party's door-step. Some people heeded this advice, others did not. And it was with all this wisdom clear in our minds that Valma and I decided to consider something we had always believed was fundamentally wrong.

Our ARMS sisters in Victoria did not necessarily share Adelaide's conservative views about how best to contact an adopted adult. ARMS Victoria had been the trailblazers in adoption and the images of them protesting in the streets of Melbourne to get rights for themselves and their children were still vivid and potent. It did not take much to convince Valma and me that direct contact with an adopted person was not something we should rule out altogether, particularly when we were so close to where she lived.

When we had a chance to talk alone we discussed the pros and cons of visiting Valma's daughter unannounced, and we repeated to one another that this was not the way ARMS in South Australia did things. But gradually we convinced ourselves that we were not at home. We were in Melbourne and things were different here. We talked about what the consequences would be if we just got in the car and drove to Valma's daughter's house. And we thought about all the people we had told back home that it was never all right just to turn up on someone's doorstep. But here we were, still thinking about doing it ourselves. We discussed it for hours – and hours.

There was no point at which we came to the view that what we were about to do was now somehow right. We simply decided we would do it. It was too cruel to tell Valma that she must never lay eyes on the child she had lost all those years ago. And if seeing her grown-up daughter for just a minute was all she was ever going to have, then right or wrong she wanted to do it. And I wanted to support her in doing it. My wish to help my dear friend was in the end stronger than any argument that this was somehow morally repugnant. So when Valma asked if I would drive her to the house and stay with her while she saw her daughter I did not hesitate in answering that I would.

The hour-long drive seemed to take forever but eventually we turned off the main road and drove down a long dirt stretch with rich farmland on either side. We did not speak to one another. There was nothing to say. We were not going to try and justify our actions. We knew we would be judged as hypocrites by some, including ourselves, and others would marvel at how Valma had lasted so long without going to the house. We just knew that at last she was going to see her daughter for the first time and although it was terrifying, it was also incredibly exciting.

When we got to the property we approached a young man who said that his wife had gone out but she would be back shortly. We did not tell him why we were there. We politely excused ourselves and drove back up to the road where we sat in the car for what seemed like hours. It was probably only about fifteen minutes.

Eventually we saw the telltale puffs of dust indicating that a car was approaching, and as it drove past the occupants looked over to see who was sitting so conspicuously on the side of the quiet dirt road. We stared back and watched them disappear down the driveway opposite us. Valma's daughter was home. I felt so scared I thought I was going to be sick. Valma looked calm and serene.

We knocked on the door and a young woman in her thirties answered. We introduced ourselves by name and Valma's daughter, seemingly unsurprised, graciously invited us into the kitchen where her husband and her adoptive mother were standing. The man smiled but the elderly lady looked ashen. The likeness between Valma and her daughter was uncanny and I was, again, struck by the similarity of voices and gestures between mothers and children who had never met before. I felt like I was seeing Valma at a younger age, a weird feeling, and I couldn't help staring at this gorgeous woman who was my friend's daughter.

We were only in the house a few minutes when the woman's adoptive mother rushed outside. I could see that Valma's daughter was concerned about not hurting anyone, and that although she was interested in Valma she also wanted to comfort her mother. She was a nice young woman and I felt sorry for her, and for a moment I really wished we had not come.

I left Valma and her daughter in the kitchen and followed the lady out to where she was taking clothes off the line and putting them into a basket. She was angry and immensely threatened by Valma's and my presence and there was no way I was going to be able to console her. I told her that I was sorry we had distressed her but she didn't answer. In the end I realised I was making matters worse by standing there and that I should just leave her alone.

I came back inside to where Valma was being introduced to her grandchildren. The young woman looked at me. It was obvious she was worried about her adoptive mother and that we were not going to be invited to sit down for a cup of tea. After a few more minutes we thanked her for allowing us to come unannounced and we left.

Valma was on cloud nine and thought it had gone very well.

She had met her daughter, her daughter's husband, and her grandchildren. And we had not been thrown out. I could understand her excitement and I did not want to tell her that I was not sure it had gone well at all. Not in the long term anyway.

Unlike the quiet trip out to the farm, the drive back into Melbourne was an intense recounting of the day's events. Valma could see that her daughter looked like her and the grandchildren were just delightful. She thought it a pity the adoptive mother was upset but that was to be expected. All in all she thought the visit had gone remarkably well and she had a good feeling about the future of their relationship.

Like Valma, I thought her daughter behaved exceptionally well under difficult circumstances. She obviously did not want to hurt Valma's feelings and she seemed genuinely interested in talking to her and introducing her to the family. But equally I saw a daughter's concern for the mother who had raised her and a need to protect her from hurt. And, of course, we had turned up unannounced against the young woman's wishes, and it was certainly not respectful of her feelings. I was not sure that, all things considered, she was going to feel as warmly towards Valma in the long run as Valma was hoping.

The next day Valma was asked by a prominent Victorian newspaper to give an interview on adoption matters in general, and excited by the previous day's events she mentioned that she had just met her daughter. She did not identify her daughter or where she lived but the young woman was deeply offended by the perceived breach of privacy. The thank you gift Valma had sent her was returned along with a note saying that she was never to make contact again.

Valma tried to explain her actions to her daughter over the following years and each time it ended with a firm rejection. When she received the Order of Australia for her work in adoption a friend contacted her daughter to let her know about her mother's achievements. The friend received a curt reply and another request that Valma leave her alone. Valma and I have often gone over the events of that day, including our decision to go against what we had always believed was the right thing to do. And on looking back at it neither of us regrets it, although we may have different reasons for coming to that conclusion.

Valma has wondered if her daughter might have eventually decided to meet her if it had not been for us turning up in the way we did. She has also thought that if she had not mentioned meeting her daughter in the press interview whether that might have made a difference. Perhaps it was something else she did, or did not do, that defined how the relationship was going to be. Or maybe it was simply one of those situations where nothing was going to change the fact that the young woman did not want to know her mother. Maybe it was all of the above. In any event, Valma has always said she was glad she met her daughter and her grandchildren. She still hopes that one day she will receive a call to say that one, or all of them, would like to get to know her properly.

For me, it was a momentous experience and I have never entirely come to terms with what we did that day. We did not agree with it and yet we did it anyway. It taught me that we are just human beings after all, and that sometimes people will do things they thought they would never do, and that they will do them because something else has become more important. And despite all my misgivings I do not regret taking my friend to meet her daughter. Valma had given so much of herself to so many mothers over the years. She was unselfish with her time and she put everyone else first. When she left ARMS to work for Jigsaw she treated adopted people, adoptive parents and mothers and fathers with equal care and concern. She was my mentor and my friend. And when she asked for my help I gave it freely. Having said that, I cannot imagine a circumstance where I would ever consider doing it again.

17

ARMS Speaks Out

IT BECAME CLEAR to ARMS after hearing more and more mothers' personal accounts that many consents had been taken improperly. Often women had given consent to adoption under extreme duress, and some had not been told their rights about revoking consent. Tens of thousands of women were refused the right to see their babies even though they had not yet signed a consent form. And girls as young as fifteen were signing consent forms even though they were still, by law, minors and not supposed to sign a legally binding document. (The legal age of adulthood was eventually dropped from twenty-one to eighteen because Australians argued, reasonably, that there was discordance between the legal age for drinking in a pub at twenty-one, and eighteen, the age young men were being conscripted to fight and die for their country in the Vietnam War.)

The section in the *Adoption of Children Act 1967* that made ARMS believe these adoptions were illegal stated that a consent to adoption was not valid if it was given under duress, or if the mother was not fully informed what it meant to give consent. ARMS now had compelling evidence to show that large numbers of women had neither freely consented, nor had they been fully informed about their rights and the implications of signing a Consent to Adoption form. And when ARMS was contacted by an Adelaide newspaper to respond to claims by Kristine Pierags, founder of Children Lost to Illegal Adoption, that many mothers were coerced into giving up their children, the response was unequivocal.

ARMS agreed there were significant questions about the legality of many of South Australia's adoptions and spoke of how mothers had pillows and sheets held up in front of them so they could not see their babies; some were not even allowed to know the gender of their child. Family and Community Services Chief Executive Officer Sue Vardon responded to the allegations and said that she was unaware of illegal adoptions but practices were sometimes less than ideal before 1972 when social workers were first appointed to handle adoptions in South Australia. It was not an admission of wrongdoing by any stretch of the imagination, but it was a public acknowledgement by the head of the Department that things had not always been done as well as perhaps they could have been. ARMS was elated.

The idea that adoptions might have been illegal hit the newspapers around Australia and mothers rang ARMS asking if it meant they might be able get their babies back. The answer, of course, was no. ARMS knew that the government would rely on what was in the best interest of the child and that the children would remain with the parents who had raised them. ARMS had never intended to suggest that children should be taken from their adoptive parents when it questioned the legality of the adoptions. Its aim was to raise awareness about the reality of adoption and show that babies were not being abandoned willy-nilly by cruel mothers lacking compassion or love for their children. ARMS wanted the community to know that adoption was not only questionable morally but there was strong evidence to suggest it was questionable legally.

The press coverage had the desired effect of getting people talking about whether some consents might not have been valid and ARMS in Victoria rang to say that the head of their Community Service Department had publicly said he believed it was likely that some adoptions were, in fact, illegal. He was a man well before his time. These were words ARMS would not hear uttered again officially for another twenty-five years. Nevertheless, for a while the community did get to hear the words *illegal* and *adoption* in the same sentence and governments did not deny the accusation outright.

Once adoption was on the political agenda, the South Australian Government was much more interested in what ARMS was saying when it took to the airwaves. The Department was, as any public servant would know, not always able to speak openly and frankly on an issue. ARMS on the other hand had very little to lose and everything to gain by speaking its mind to anyone who would listen, and now and then one of its spokespeople got into just a little bit of hot water.

Valma was having one of those frustrating days where nothing was going right and she was not sure ARMS was going to succeed in getting equal rights for mothers in the new Adoption Act. People had been full of promises but there was a concerted effort from the anti-law-change groups saying that mothers must not be given their children's names and that it would ruin people's lives if the records were opened. Some of the old myths about girls abandoning their babies and only wanting them back now that the hard work had been done were reappearing in letters to the editor. And then there were the hostile phone calls that usually went to Valma's phone number as the chairperson of ARMS. It was at the end of one of *those* days that Valma was bailed up by a very friendly and amiable journalist asking to have an informal and off-the-record discussion.

Valma was generally canny, but this day she did not remember the golden rule: *There is no such thing as an off-the-record discussion with a journalist.* And so she let fly, saying a few not so nice things about people she had trusted and whom she had now come to believe were not allies of ARMS at all. Fortunately she did not name names but she did suggest fairly strongly that these were untrustworthy people who did not tell the truth. Of course it was far too interesting an interview to remain *off the record* and the next day her words appeared verbatim in the newspaper, to the horror of ARMS, Valma, and the Minister for Community Welfare.

John Cornwall was not big in stature but he was certainly big in voice. He was a formidable man and ARMS had, up until now, had a good relationship with him and his staff. He was gentle with us when we were making our sometimes muddled submission to the

Select Committee. He had also indicated that he and his government were listening to ARMS and that it would do all it could to recognise mothers' issues in the new Adoption Act. And now ARMS had made him furious.

Dr Cornwall knew ARMS was not speaking about him in the article. He was angry because ARMS was not known for going off half-cocked, making off-the-cuff and libellous statements to the media. The Minister had come to have some faith in ARMS's views and he felt betrayed and, although he did not say it, he was probably a little nervous about what ARMS might do next. ARMS had become the loudest voice in South Australia when it came to mothers' issues. People were intrigued by what these women looked like and they were amazed when they found out they were their next-door neighbours, teachers, doctors, politicians, friends, relatives – and their own mothers. And most of all people were captured by the believability of the women's stories. ARMS mothers were passionate, but they were also credible. And now this!

A ministerial assistant rang ARMS and said that the Minister had just read the daily paper and he wanted to see Valma and me *now*. I was terrified. I had heard he could be blistering when he was angry. Valma took it in her stride. We had not sat down before John Cornwall's usually smooth forehead wrinkled with rage and he blasted Valma and me for our idiocy. He asked us what on earth we were thinking, particularly given the government had been doing everything possible to get mothers equal rights – something the other States had to date ruled out. He pushed the offending newspaper across his desk and said he simply could not believe what he had read and that he just hoped we had not damaged our chances irreparably. His adviser, who had also been extremely supportive of our cause, stood beside him and looked at us with a mixture of disappointment that we could have been so stupid and pity at what we were now enduring.

I was weak at the knees, but instead of Valma apologising to Dr Cornwall she went on the attack. She asked him, rhetorically, what could he expect when mothers had been treated so badly for so long? I could not believe my ears and I looked up to see if the blood vessels in the Minister's face were about to burst. Instead, he started to smile. Valma went on to say that she had been speaking of the past in her interview, not about people in the current Department for Community Welfare. She emphasised she had been taken out of context. Neither of us mentioned that Valma had been duped into thinking she was speaking to a journalist *off the record!* I just stood there thinking that this could easily have happened to me.

Dr Cornwall asked us to sit down and in a much warmer voice told us that we needed to be very careful about what we said to the media from now on. He leaned forward and said, as if in confidence, that we probably did not know it yet but ARMS was now a powerful voice. It had the ability to gain a lot of public support, and therefore political alliance, for mothers' rights. But if ARMS acted rashly it could destroy any hope of getting favourable legislation in the forthcoming Adoption Act. He was right. ARMS did not really know how influential it had become. It seemed only yesterday that mothers were fighting for just a morsel of information about their children and now ARMS stood at the forefront of the adoption debate as to whether mothers should be included in the new Bill. The Minister reminded us that we had been listened to because we were not radical militants threatening anarchy if we did not get what we wanted. We were believed because we were just ordinary women telling our stories simply and honestly. He urged us to stay focused and not to go off the rails when we were so close to victory.

Valma and I left the meeting knowing we had escaped lightly and that we, and ARMS, needed to learn from our near miss. Our goal was to tell as many people as possible what had happened to mothers, using every opportunity to get the message out. ARMS had been very successful in putting adoption on the agenda and, in particular, raising the profile of mothers in the process. Adoption was a hot topic now and ARMS was caught up in the scramble between politics and the media. It was time to be discerning, to pick its moments carefully, and avoid becoming the meat in the sandwich. Dr Cornwall's wrath, albeit fleeting, made us realise that whilst ARMS was being sought out for its opinion on all things adoption its position was tenuous and its credibility could slide into the abyss if its representatives did not act wisely and with caution.

After the dust had settled Valma and I agreed with the Minister's request to run any press releases past his adviser before they were released. (Of course, this was an arrangement that would only last until the Bill giving mothers equal rights was in the bag.) And privately we agreed never again to believe a journalist who told us, 'Don't worry. This is off the record.'

18

Tears in Parliament House

IN THE LAST MONTH OF WINTER 1988, ARMS received news that knocked mothers off their feet. Dr Cornwall was leaving Parliament. An emergency management committee meeting was held. There was a fear of having to start campaigning again or risk losing the battle for mothers to be recognised equally in the new Adoption Act. It had not been easy winning John Cornwall over. He did not suffer fools gladly and it had taken some time for ARMS to earn his serious consideration. But he had come on board and he was sympathetic to ARMS's view that birth parents and adult adopted people should be given the same rights to receive identifying information about one another. ARMS was extremely worried about who was going to step into his shoes.

Susan Lenehan took over John Cornwall's portfolio as Minister for Community Welfare. It was one of a number of roles she had in the South Australian Parliament. Lenehan was known as a livewire and described as a professional who saw her femininity as a strength to be celebrated rather than hidden. ARMS had met her when it lobbied women from both the major parties. She was dynamic and gutsy, but little was known about just how far she would go to support mothers in the matter of giving them the right to apply for identifying information about their children.

ARMS did not know that Susan was, in fact, familiar with issues for mothers. Corinne had been the Minister's assistant at her electorate office for some years and she had lost a baby through adoption when she was young. Corinne had talked with Susan about what it was like to have been a young country girl sent to the city to be shut away in an unmarried mothers' home during her pregnancy. Susan heard how girls in the home were made to do physically gruelling work to earn their keep – things that would never be expected of a pregnant woman in other circumstance – and that after a thirty-seven-hour labour, and a delivery that remains a blank in Corinne's memory, her baby was bundled up and taken away. Corinne told Susan about the drive back to the home and how she tried to peek at her baby held tauntingly just out of reach in the Matron's arms. And that she only saw her child once after that, for a few minutes before she left the home forever.

Corinne was not trying to gain sympathy by telling her story. She was simply stating it as it was. But for Susan it was shocking and unacceptable and she vowed that something must be done to change Australia's archaic adoption laws.

Susan Lenehan proved to be as committed as her predecessor to changing the legislation to include mothers, and ARMS could not have been given a better advocate to take John Cornwall's place.

One issue that caused much discussion and debate in Parliament and in the media was the matter of a veto. Dr Cornwall had not pressed for one when he was Minister but Opposition newcomer Diana Laidlaw was deeply concerned about the rights of those who did not want information divulged and she led a strong push for a veto provision to be included in the new Adoption Act. Some members wanted a veto which had to be renewed every five years and where identifying information would be given to the person requesting it if the veto lapsed. Others supported the view that the veto should be lifelong. They did not see why people should have to come back every few years to reaffirm their original decision. And some adoptive parents wanted to be able to place a veto on their adopted children's behalf because they had never told them they were adopted.

These were all legitimate issues and for months newspaper articles discussed the pros and cons of the veto and interested parties argued vehemently about what should be given to whom and how best the State could protect people's privacy. And as the war raged ARMS waited with bated breath to see what this new Minister for Community Welfare was going to ask Parliament to consider.

On 8 September 1988, Susan Lenehan stepped into the House of Assembly and moved that the Bill for an Act to provide for the adoption of children and to repeal the *Adoption of Children Act 1967* be read for a second time. The Minister for Community Welfare caught the members' attention when she said that adoption touched the lives of thousands of people in South Australia and that there would be few who did not know an adoptive parent, an adopted person, or a birth mother or father. Her audience listened intently when she spoke of the deliberations of the 1987 Select Committee and that 'perhaps the most sensitive aspect of the proposed changes in the original Bill was the provision for adopted people and birth parents to have access to information about each other upon the adopted persons reaching the age of 18 years'. And having demonstrated the importance of the Bill before the House, Susan went on to outline other areas that had been hotly debated by the Committee, including the provision for single people and de facto couples to adopt children.

The Minister concluded her speech by thanking her predecessor, the Hon. John Cornwall. And in a strong voice demonstrating her unwavering conviction that this was a right and proper piece of legislation she looked across the House and said, 'I believe [the Bill] has achieved a good balance between the indisputable rights of adopted people and birth parents to information about their origins or the children they placed and the need to protect the privacy of individuals who may not wish their present lives to be disrupted by their past.'

The sheer length of the explanation of the Adoption Bill meant some aspects were left for members to read in Hansard. Among them were references to ARMS representation at the Select Committee concerning mothers not being fully informed about the implications of giving consent to adoption. The Bill proposed that consent could not be taken until at least three days after the parent/s had been counselled about what adoption meant and that, in usual circumstances, consent could not occur within fourteen days of the child's birth. Furthermore, a witness to the consent must not be the same person who counselled the parent/s and the witness must be satisfied the parent/s understood the implications of signing consent and the process for revoking it.

The Bill was what ARMS had hoped for, and much more than it had expected. And it was passed without alteration to the section giving mothers equal rights with adopted adults to apply for identifying information. Now all that was needed was for it to get through the Legislative Council.

ARMS got the word that the Adoption Bill was going to be heard in the Legislative Council on 9 November 1988. If it passed, future adoptions would no longer be secret affairs. New mothers and fathers would be able to have identifying information and contact with their children up until they were five years old, and beyond if the adoptive parents agreed to it. Open adoption would become the standard procedure for all future permanent child placements and de facto couples and individuals would be eligible to adopt.

For past adoptions, birth mothers – and fathers where registered – would be able to apply for identifying information about their children and the same right would apply to adopted adults. A veto would be included in the Bill, and it must be renewed every five years. No one other than the adopted adult or birth parent/s named on the original birth certificate could place a veto on the release of identifying information.

ARMS held its breath because it knew that if mothers were given the same rights as their children it would be a first in Australia, and a first in any English-speaking country that had had secret adoption legislation. Scotland and England had given adopted adults the right to their original birth certificates, but no one in the United Kingdom, Ireland, the United States, Canada, South Africa or New Zealand was prepared to take the chance on giving mothers the same rights. If this section of the Act was passed, it would be history making.

Valma, Rhonda and a number of other mothers from ARMS met in the Gallery of Parliament House with their friends from Parents of Adoptees and Jigsaw. The groups had worked long and hard and they were weary from campaigning. But they were also excited about the fact that the day had finally come when the Bill would be passed by the Legislative Council.

The Australian Democrats held the balance of power in the Legislative Council but no one expected debate from its leader Ian Gilfillan and Legislative Counsellor Michael Elliott. There had been general agreement between the major parties that the Bill was reasonable and it was simply a matter of it being passed by the Council, proclaimed in early 1989 and enacted in around July of the same year. However, the Australian Democrats Party had a Bill of its own and its members were determined to get it through Parliament.

The 1980s marked a time in global history when countries were becoming increasingly aware of the effects of Western society's lifestyle on the world. Global warming was gaining credibility as an issue and a growing hole in the ozone layer could no longer be ignored. Major contributors to the looming environmental catastrophe were chlorofluorocarbons found in most spray cans used around the home, and the Democrats had developed a solid piece of legislation banning their use. It was a proposal that had caused much controversy but it was also vital to the world's future, and in order to get it passed the Australian Democrats did something that enraged the Parliament and everyone sitting upstairs in the Gallery. When the Adoption Bill came up for discussion the Democrats refused to look at it until the other parties agreed to pass its own Bill banning the use of chlorofluorocarbons.

Yells of horror rang out across the Gallery and Valma and several other mothers rushed down the stairs in tears. They had waited for most of their adult lives to hear the news that mothers might have the right to find their children, only to have it stopped at the last hurdle by a political party holding everyone to ransom. Well, that was how ARMS saw it. And so did the media in reports over the following days.

Democrat Michael Elliott said he accepted he was not the most popular person in the world after the vote, especially as some women wept openly in front of him. The Democrats were, however, simply making a point and the Bill would still be passed by Christmas.

Over the next days the Democrats were called undemocratic and their actions hailed as akin to blackmail as they held up the functions of Parliament for ulterior motives. Nevertheless, there seemed to be little understanding about the reason for the distress felt by those in the Gallery. After all the Bill would be passed in time for it to be enacted in July 1989.

ARMS was incensed. When the media wanted to know what the mothers thought about the delay in passing the Bill there was a swift and impassioned response. ARMS said its mothers were being kicked around like a political football to serve the needs of a few people on a minority issue. Of course, it was a knee-jerk response and no one at ARMS really believed the hole in the ozone layer was a 'minority issue'. But neither did it see why the two matters could not be resolved simultaneously. And in regard to the belief that there was no reason for mothers to be crying in Parliament because the Bill was soon to be passed anyway, ARMS reply was equally biting. Clearly people had no idea how long mothers had waited already; for some more than fifty years. And neither did anyone seem to understand how groundbreaking this piece of legislation was, and that until it was passed ARMS could not relax.

Seven days later, on 16 November 1988, the Bill was finally passed as ARMS mothers sat in the Gallery gripping one another in anticipation. As they came down the stairs buzzing with excitement they were asked if they would like to share a fizzy drink with some of the members of Parliament to celebrate the historical achievement.

It would not be the last time that an historic day for mothers in Parliament House would be overshadowed by political manoeuvring. But that was a long way off and for the moment ARMS was just glad it had taken a chance on fighting for mothers, and that

South Australia had had the wisdom to listen and the courage to do what was right.

Over 12,000 adoptions had occurred in South Australia since the 1920s, and Adoption Services reported that by June 1989, 5100 people had registered to receive identifying information about their lost relative. Only 289 had vetoed.

ARMS did not know it then, but it would play an integral role in the distribution of identifying information to applicants, and in supporting families through whatever they might find when the secret records were, at last, opened.

19

Secrets Revealed

IT SEEMED LIKE ALL of ARMS's dreams had come true. Firstly laws had been passed in South Australia, not only giving adopted adults the right to apply for identifying information but, miraculously, giving the same right to mothers as well. Then, to cap off a phenomenal year, ARMS heard it was to be one of the groups in 1989 to benefit from a $2.2 million funding initiative designed to kick-start non-government organisations providing vital support services to the community. The funding meant that ARMS would now be able to employ a co-ordinator to oversee the running of the agency, and pay for a new typewriter and a photocopier.

As Susan Lenehan proudly handed over the cheque to Valma, the management committee and members gaped in amazement. ARMS would become the first adoption support group in Australian history to receive government funding to provide a professional counselling service to people affected by adoption. The mothers did not know it yet but their little support group was about to change forever. And it would be a mixed blessing.

The management committee advertised for a co-ordinator and Valma resigned as chairperson and put in an application for the job. Everyone celebrated when she received the letter notifying her she had been successful and that she would become ARMS first paid co-ordinator.

In line with the new laws the government established an office separate from Adoption Services specifically to handle applications and vetoes and the Family Information Service became for many years the agency with which ARMS worked most closely. Jigsaw, a newly formed Adoptee Support Group, and Lila's Adoptive Parents group were also invited to become part of the new strategy to bring non-government agencies, support groups and government departments together to work collaboratively towards a common goal.

By the late 1980s there were relatively few adoptions (they had dropped by fifty per cent within three years of the introduction of the single mothers benefit in 1973, and by seventy-five per cent by 1984) and it was anticipated that the vast majority would be *open adoptions* where mothers and fathers, adoptive families and children would share information and ideally have contact with one another. In line with this new way of placing children the government decided that prospective adoptive parents might benefit from attending workshops where they could listen to the experiences of mothers who had given children up for adoption as well as those of adopted adults and adoptive parents. It was a brave initiative.

Maureen had been an ARMS member for a couple of years and she was now ensconced on the management committee – a role she would bravely assume for the next twenty-two years – and along with several other mothers she volunteered to tell her story to the young couples. Maureen was a considerate woman who was very clear about her own experience. She was also aware that these young people were excited about getting their new babies and it was important that a balanced, if perhaps somewhat detached, view of the mother's experience might be the most sensitive way to handle these workshops. She was of course right. It was important to tell the about-to-be parents that not all mothers had had a positive experience losing their babies through adoption, but it was equally important not to dump mothers' emotional baggage onto these young people who just wanted a baby they could call their own. Maureen was a great communicator, perceptive and intelligent about her audience, and it was to her credit that the groups dispersed feeling more knowledgeable about mothers but not so uncomfortable that they could not come up to her in the tea-break and ask her more questions.

But being 'mum' at the sessions was not for everyone. Some of the volunteer mothers said they felt strangely guilty after the workshops. There they were, telling their stories of loss and grief, and at the same time feeling excited for the young people who were eagerly anticipating getting their babies – babies who would, most likely, cause their own mothers the same feelings of loss and grief the ARMS mothers had felt. The women came to understand the term *cognitive dissonance* – being able to hold two opposing views at the same time – and after a while the volunteers accepted that in this odd world of adoption they did not need to feel guilty if they were sad for the mothers who had lost their children but happy for the young couples who were about to get theirs.

In the first months after the new law changes Family Information Service attempted to manage all the applications. Fees were paid in three stages during the application process. The first fee of $50 was paid when the application was registered. The second fee of $75 was to pay for a search to be undertaken and the third fee of $50 was to receive the information. People who proved they could not afford the $175 fee could apply for a waiver.

In the early days each applicant was seen by a social worker to help the person deal with issues that might arise along the way to getting, or not getting, identifying information. Eventually the Service realised that it would have a waiting list nearly as long as Victoria's if it did not adapt to the growing demand. It discontinued the routine interviews and started offering applicants the opportunity of receiving their information in a group, individually through the Service, or with an independent counsellor. And, here again, some people from the adoption support groups proved to be invaluable in this capacity.

The independent counsellors were self-employed people chosen and trained by Family Information Service to meet with the applicants and give them the identifying information they had requested. The prospect of giving people information they had wanted for so long was exciting and rewarding, but the counsellors also had another role. They had to assess each situation and make the decision whether or not the applicant should be given the information without first seeing a government social worker. ARMS independent counsellors said that only rarely did they withhold identifying information until the person saw someone from the Family Information Service. And when they did, it was generally because the applicant was unrealistic about contact, or she or he had unresolved issues that might get in the way of a reunion if they were not addressed.

Where applicants met in groups to get their identifying information – usually around fifteen people per group – part of the process was to prepare them for what they might find in the big manila envelope they were about to receive, and how they might best go about approaching the other party. It was strongly recommended that they should use a third party to make contact and that they ought not just go up and knock on the stranger's door. (Valma and I would cringe when this was mentioned, and it would be a long time before we would tell anyone about our little trip into the Victorian countryside.)

At the group sessions adoption support people spoke about what to expect on the search and reunion journey and some of the applicants wanted to talk to an ARMS mother after they had opened their envelopes. Some adoptees were keen to know what their own mothers might be like and how they should approach them to get the best outcome. Some mothers had just seen the names of their children for the first time and they wanted to talk to another mother because they had never spoken about their experience before. And then there were others, mothers and adopted people alike, who left the meeting quietly with tears in their eyes. They preferred to sit in the car park on their own when they opened the envelope.

Once people had received their identifying information ARMS was one of the agencies they could use to handle the initial contact. Not only did a lot of mothers use the service but a surprising number of adopted adults also approached ARMS to find their parents. They said they thought their mothers might be more amenable to an approach from a group run by women who had shared the same story, rather than by a government department some had seen as instrumental in taking the babies in the first place. Whatever the reasons, ARMS became a popular service for conducting reunions and almost as soon as the laws changed the phones began ringing off the hook.

No one at ARMS really knew how the business of search, contact and reunion was going to work out on such a large scale and whether or not the agency had the capacity to deal with the difficult situations that lay ahead. In the past, searches had been laborious and positive matches were few and far between. Even among the few who had made contact there had been a fair share of sad stories and stern refusals. And then there was the added responsibility of staff, wages, occupational health and safety, audits, more submission-writing, keeping case notes. And of course ARMS was still operating from Valma's home and the office was cramped and becoming more impossible by the day. It was a far cry from the early days when women sat in a circle at the Women's Information Switchboard asking questions about how their children might look and if they were alive and happy with their new families.

But it was also the stuff that dreams are made of. Mothers were finding their children after twenty, thirty, forty, even fifty years. Sons and daughters were getting the chance for the first time to find out the truth behind their adoptions; that they had not been abandoned or forgotten. Fathers were coming back on the scene and saying they were sorry; it was the beginning of their healing too. And many more adoptive parents than might have been expected were embracing their new extended families, happy that their children could now put to rest the agony of not knowing who they were.

ARMS was on a sharp learning curve.

20

Professionalising ARMS

THE EARLY YEARS after the law changes were exhilarating but challenging. The support group numbers swelled significantly and it was decided to keep a central location at the Women's Information Switchboard for most of the meetings and only do individual counselling and contact preparation at the ARMS office, still operating out of Valma's house.

A lot of work was done over the telephone and ARMS now had a facsimile machine, which meant that written material could be shared between agencies more quickly than by general post. (Computers, the internet, email and mobile phones were still years off!) ARMS had also received some funding for a new word processor, which meant that anyone using it could review what was written before it was typed onto the actual page. Letters not only looked more professional but spelling and grammar were more accurate as well. All this was important because ARMS was now conferring with government agencies around Australia, the United Kingdom, New Zealand and the United States. It was no longer an independent but poor self-help support group. Now it could (and according to its funding agreement, was *required* to) employ staff and provide a government-endorsed service, and that gave it a whole new status with many benefits – and an equal number of headaches. ARMS had to work out how to keep its grass roots integrity and at the same time learn to work with government to provide the unique service it was so good at delivering.

Some people thought that by taking the government's money

ARMS had lost its independence and the criticism was countered by the question – albeit rhetorical – who better than mothers to train professionals to work with mothers in their own service? Mothers in ARMS were taking control of their lives. In the past they had no control and no power, and they saw professionals make ill-informed (and some would say illegal) decisions on their behalf. Now they were training professionals to work for them and they were educating them and their peers about the reality of adoption and what it was that mothers needed now. It was true that being funded came at a price and only the future would tell if ARMS was going to lose more than it would gain by accepting the money and everything that came with it.

ARMS had to professionalise its service because of the people it was now there to help. It was no small responsibility being the mediator between two people for whom a reunion meant everything, or counselling a mother who had learned her child had died thirty years before. The variations in experience were as diverse as in any population.

The matter of establishing contact on behalf of a mother or an adopted adult was complex and highly charged for everyone involved. When ARMS was asked to make an approach on behalf of a mother, Valma first met with the woman to see what her expectations of contact, short term and long term, might be. She listened quietly when mothers said that all they wanted to do was count their child's fingers and toes. She understood that for them it was as if time had stood still and they would not be able to move forward until they had done the things that had been denied them when their babies were born.

Val nodded when women said they knew they could not assume the role of mother and that all they wanted was to be friends with their now grown-up children. She suspected that in some cases the mothers actually did want to be the mother, but at least they were heading in the right direction by knowing a special friendship was a much more likely outcome.

Occasionally a mother talked about how she *just knew* that her child would be delighted to meet her and that she was equally sure they would pick up where they left off all those years ago. Val spent extra time talking about the reality of a reunion with these mothers. The truth was that not all adopted adults were interested in meeting their mothers and some were downright angry and hostile about any approach. There were people who had never been told they were adopted. They would have to deal with all the emotions associated with finding out the truth before they could even consider developing a relationship with their mothers, if at all. It could be hard convincing a mother that her dreams and hopes were nothing more than that, and that contact came in many shapes and forms. Most mothers got the general idea but after the reunion, almost without exception, they said that nothing could really prepare them for meeting their children and it had been different from anything they had imagined.

When the laws changed there was no specialised counselling model for working with mothers, either with respect to the unusual kind of grief they experienced (their children were gone, not missing, nor dead as far as they knew) or for mothers who were about to meet their children for the first time. It had only been a few years since Robin Winkler and Margaret van Keppel had published their seminal work on relinquishing mothers and determined that they experienced debilitating unresolved grief due to losing their babies. But grief counselling was still geared towards people who had lost someone through death and therapists were only just starting to think about grief and loss relating to missing children who were never found. No one really knew what was going to eventuate when thousands of women met the children they had never known but had grieved for, in some cases, for over fifty years.

ARMS could not look to its peers interstate or overseas for help either. None of the other English-speaking countries had given mothers the rights South Australia had, and although Victoria's Department for Community Welfare had been making approaches to adopted adults on behalf of mothers, its issues were a little different. In that State adopted people could get the original birth certificate and mothers could not veto its release. Mothers did not have a legal right to identifying information but they could ask the Department to approach their children for them. The Department had the final say as to whether it would do an outreach, and if it did and the adopted person, or in some circumstances the adoptive parents, did not want contact the mother would only be given non-identifying information about her child. The priority in Victoria was the adopted adult and given its huge waiting list to provide information and conduct searches, it was not in a position to provide comprehensive counselling to every woman affected by adoption. Eventually a non-government agency called Vanish would be set up to meet the ongoing needs of people affected by adoption in Victoria but that was still in the future; in the meantime ARMS client numbers were increasing in size, and complexity, by the day.

Valma worked at ARMS for nearly two years as its first paid co-ordinator and the end of her employment did not come easily for her, or for the management committee. She would not be the only mother to move from being a committee member to becoming an employee, and to leave because the tensions between the old role and the new one could not be resolved amicably. Fingers were pointed and accusations were made on both sides and in the end Valma resigned. It had been a huge part of her life for eight years and her contributions were many, some groundbreaking. If it had not been for Valma it is unlikely ARMS would have fought for the rights of mothers in Parliament in 1988 making world history. She had a vision about what ARMS could provide to people and she was there to see it become the first adoption group in Australia, probably the world, to receive funding to provide a comprehensive counselling and support service to mothers. And she had a political nose that was next to none. She knew how to get governments on board and, crucially, how to keep them there. Of course she could also be difficult, as marvellous people often are, and there were times when ARMS's frustration with her was only matched by her own self-criticism. But most of all, she was brave. When Valma came to ARMS she was too scared to use her own name in public.

Her fear was every bit as profound as any other mother who had been excommunicated from family, friends and society and who was made to pay the ultimate price by giving her child to strangers. But in spite of her own terrors she stood up, said her name out loud, and swore to help mothers like herself. And that takes true courage.

After a short rest Valma joined Jigsaw where she worked primarily as its president until she retired in her seventies. During that time she also managed to complete a degree in Women's Studies, a graduate diploma in Group Work and a masters in Social Sciences. On 26 January 2006, Valma was awarded an Order of Australia for her tireless work helping all people affected by adoption. No book written about the mothers in ARMS could be done without acknowledging her place in its incredible history.

21

A Cottage in Hackney

I WAS WORKING in a large psychiatric hospital as a base grade social worker when I got the call from Loryn asking if I would consider applying for the job as ARMS co-ordinator and social worker. I was dying to get out of the job I was in – I loved the clients but I had been a whistleblower and my name was mud among some of the staff there – and the idea that I might work with mothers on an issue I felt passionate about was appealing. I put everything I had into the application and the interview and after a few tense days I was told I had the job.

One of the immediate problems was the issue of an office. Along with the loss of Valma, ARMS now had to find alternative accommodation. It was not long before Loryn said she had found the ideal spot on North Terrace in Hackney. It was the front two rooms of a single-fronted house on the same Adelaide street as Government House, the Art Gallery, Museum, University of Adelaide, Royal Adelaide Hospital and the Botanical Gardens, but just outside Adelaide's central business district significantly reducing the rent. It was within walking distance of all the major city services and it had the North Terrace name, making it extremely easy to find. The management committee snapped up the property and then went about the task of finding furniture to fill the two rooms.

The little cottage that would become ARMS's home for the next seven years was a typical turn-of-the-century inner-city house. The single-gabled roof jutted up behind a bull-nose veranda that hung over a tiny unkempt garden. The front door opened onto a wide hallway that ran the full length of the house but was blocked halfway by a white plasterboard panel. On the other side of the barrier lived a quiet man who rode a bicycle and shared the outside toilet with the front tenant.

The first room had a small white porcelain sink tucked away in one corner near an art nouveau green tiled fireplace. The room was clean and light with a good-sized bay window. The second room, of equal ample size, was known as the 'counselling room'. It also ran off the large hallway and its window faced out onto a narrow path that led to the outhouse at the back of the property. This room had 1950s style built-in cupboards covering an entire wall with a mirror in the centre – perfect for storing all ARMS records, and the vacuum cleaner.

The hallway was the perfect size for a couple of chairs and a coffee table, and the all-important photocopier at the far end near the partition. The furniture came from Salvation Army shops around town and the management committee made sure they bought a couple of particularly comfy chairs to go in the counselling room. It would not be long before there were not enough chairs or space to accommodate the growing number of women coming to the group meetings but that problem would have to wait. At least ARMS now had a home again.

I had learned by now that as a therapist it might be handy to have a counselling model to follow. I looked for something that might fit the mothers' experience but I was unsuccessful. These mothers were not victims of crime, nor had they committed one; their children were not dead and nor were they missing; these women were not really even mothers – not in the traditional sense anyway. And yet they described all the emotions of unresolved grief, loss, guilt, shame and anger that one might expect to see with any of the above experiences. And so I naively developed my own eight-stage pre- and post-relinquishment counselling model. I did not bother to copyright it – it was not really that good. But it was a start.

The model aimed to do several things. Firstly, it was to help mothers understand their own experience in the broader sociological and political context, not just within their own narrow frame of reference as girls who were single and whose family did not support them because of their sexual transgression. It was amazing how quickly they cottoned on to the fact that what they thought was their own decision was shaped by a whole lot of other factors and that sometimes they were being presented with Hobson's Choice; that is a free choice in which only one option is being offered!

Secondly, the counselling was to encourage the mothers to talk about anything and everything associated with the pregnancy, the delivery, the relinquishment, and the years living with the loss and, for many, the secret. These were experiences many mothers had never talked about – with anyone. They had been told to go away and get on with their lives and that they would soon forget about what had happened to them.

Thirdly, the model was a tool to give mothers the opportunity to express in a safe place all the feelings they had suppressed for years. They were encouraged to show their rage when they realised they had been punished for the very thing they had been told they must do if they loved their babies. And they cried buckets when they remembered their babies being taken from them and when they signed the forms depriving them of their parental rights forever.

And the fourth purpose for the counselling was to try and bring the mother forward in time so she could imagine her child at the age she or he would be now. It sounded odd but the reality was that many mothers still saw their children as the babies they had lost many years before and in the absence of any photos or other information that was how they still saw them. Some of these women were going to meet their children and it was important that they had an opportunity to explore the gap in time between when they saw their babies last (if they had seen them at all) and what that person might look like now – a bit like Rip van Winkle going to sleep and waking up twenty years later to find his world and everyone in it had all grown older – including himself.

Some people contacted ARMS because they had just met their

lost family member and they were unsure about what to do next. On one occasion a mother came to the office because she had just received her identifying information and had been told that her daughter could be located at a particular psychiatric hospital. The woman assumed that it was the girl's place of work and she was distraught when she learned that her child was an inpatient at the institution and that she had been there for more than twenty years. The mother wanted to see her daughter but she did not know how to go about it.

The psychiatric hospital the woman was talking about just happened to be the place where I had commenced my social work career and the daughter was someone I knew quite well. I knew that meeting her would require a great deal of courage and openness on the part of the mother, and that the hospital would not be immediately supportive of an approach from her. The adoptive family were not happy with the mother's presence and even some of the ward staff were suspicious about the woman's motives for coming back into her daughter's life after so many years. They did not realise that the mother had been prevented, by law, from doing anything sooner.

The daughter knew she was adopted and was excited about meeting her mother – it was the happiest I had ever seen her – and with help from the chief social worker the hospital chief executive eventually relented and allowed them to meet. I only saw the mother and daughter a couple of times after their reunion and I have no doubt there would have been many obstacles for them to overcome if they were going to develop some kind of meaningful relationship with one another.

A few years ago I heard that the daughter died – she was still living in the psychiatric institution she had been in since she was a teenager. It was a sad story and I thought about what it must have been like for the mother to dream of her daughter's life as being one of happy fulfilment only to have it shattered so dramatically. And then I remembered the big smile the daughter had on her face the last time I saw her. She told me that she was happy to have met her mother. And with the look of a child who has just been offered a sugary sweet she turned to me and said, 'And you know, she told me that she has always loved me. *Always* loved me.' I decided it would be that memory I would keep in my mind whenever I thought about the merits, or otherwise, of opening up secret records come what may.

Cynthia was another woman who had waited excitedly to receive information about her daughter. She had been a long-standing member of ARMS and she was well-prepared for the possibility that her thirty-year wait might be in vain and that her child might not want to know her. However, she was totally unprepared when I visited her home to tell her that her daughter had died some years earlier. As I knocked on the door I thought this was what it must be like to be a police officer having to go to someone's home and tell them that their child has died. It was a sickening feeling.

After hearing about the illness that had claimed her daughter's life Cynthia asked if the adoptive parents might consider talking to her. Knowing about Margaret's experience some years earlier I was not confident that the family would want to have anything to do with Cynthia but I agreed to contact them and ask the question.

The adoptive mother was a kind and generous person and after getting over the shock of being asked if she would consider speaking with her child's biological mother the dear lady embraced the opportunity wholeheartedly. The two mothers spoke with one another several times over the next few months and they shared information that appeared to be mutually consoling. Cynthia was able to develop a visual image of her child and the adoptive mother was able to speak to the woman who had given her daughter life. It was not exactly a happy ending but it proved that even under the most dire of circumstances two mothers could put aside their own sad loss and support one another with compassion and respect.

Sometimes reunions went relatively smoothly. Maureen, who was now ARMS chairperson, had met her daughter in 1986 and their relationship had developed into a warm friendship. Loryn was in contact with her son and Rhonda was getting to know her grandchildren. My daughter and I were having deeply philosophical discussions about how we would define our relationship – not as mother and daughter but not as friends either; something in between the two perhaps.

Getting people together was a new business. Some reunions seemed to fall into place fairly easily. Others were difficult from beginning to end. And there was a surprise around every corner, as I was about to find out.

22

Clients or Friends?

ARMS ENCOURAGED MOTHERS and adopted adults who had just received their information to go through an intermediary when the first contact was being made. Many did, but others wanted to maintain a high level of control over the process and decided to do it on their own or with the help of family or a friend. On the day I got the call from Paula and John I did not realise just how different this contact was going to be, not just in how it transpired, but also because I had not anticipated what it would feel like to facilitate a reunion for clients who were also my closest friends.

John had already dabbled at trying to find his mother. He knew his original first and middle names were Michael Joseph and I had told him that some mothers looked through the personal notices in the paper, hoping their children might celebrate a special birthday by putting their name in print and perhaps disclosing vital information that could help a search. He decided to try it, giving his date of birth and original names – the ones his mother would surely recognise – and asking if she might like to contact him.

On the big day John got the paper earlier than usual and opened the pages to the classifieds hoping his mother would be having breakfast somewhere doing the same thing. He found his personal notice giving the birth date and original names, but there was something odd about the advert that he could not quite put his finger on. As he and his wife sat down to coffee and toast the problem became apparent.

'The names your birth mother gave you were Michael Joseph, weren't they?' Paula asked.

John nodded.

'Well they've put down the name of a famous American movie star. Could you by any chance have told the newspaper your name was Michael Douglas?' his wife said, pointing at the rogue word.

John did not know whether to laugh or cry. In his nervousness he had given the newspaper a name as familiar to him as his own. He was frustrated by the fact that no one replied to his advertisement. It might have been that his mother did not see it. Or it could have been that she did read the notice and was surprised to learn that such a famous film star was adopted and was looking for his mother in Adelaide, South Australia. After giving it a bit of thought John asked if I would try and find Jennifer in a more direct way and speak with her personally. By this time I had done quite a few first contacts and without hesitating I agreed.

Doing searches for mothers and female adoptees was generally more difficult than for males because most women changed surname when they married. You could often find men by just looking them up in the phone book. When looking for women you sometimes had to contact family members and ask discretely if they knew where such-and-such a person might be now. Often the people were suspicious and wanted to know details of who you were and why they should pass on a person's whereabouts to you. Others knew exactly what the call was about and were opposed to any kind of approach. Either way, you had to be extremely careful not to disclose anything that could breach client confidentiality whilst also giving a plausible story. It was fraught with difficulty and every time I picked up the phone to make one of those calls my heart pounded and my hands shook.

If you did know the whereabouts of the person letters were generally the first means of contact. But, again, often you had no idea of the circumstances of the person you were writing to, and you had to be careful not to say too much, just in case busy bodies opened mail that was not meant for them. And of course the ARMS letterhead with its black silhouette of a mother holding the white silhouette of an absent baby in her arms could be revealing, especially if the person reading it knew what 'relinquishing' meant. If I was really worried about what I might be exposing – and that was often – I would write the letter on blank paper and keep it nondescript. Something about looking for a lost relative and please contact me if you might know this person.

As the years went on initial approaches got a bit easier because, unlike the old Contact Register that was never advertised, the new adoption laws were heavily publicised and more people knew that an approach from a long-lost relative was possible.

At first glance the prospect of finding John's mother looked good because he had Jennifer's married name. As it happened, however, she proved not to be as easy to find as we had hoped. She was not currently on the electoral roll under the name John had, and it was assumed she had either changed her name, moved interstate, or died. Fortunately I had a name and phone number of someone who might have been related to her and I thought it was worth giving the man a call – albeit a very discreet one.

With a lump in my throat, and a feeling of terror that I had not experienced in a previous contact, I dialled the number. An elderly man answered the phone and when I said who I was looking for he was most helpful. I did not even have to make up something to avoid prying questions. I simply said I was trying to get in touch with Jennifer and I wondered if they might be related. I scribbled quickly as he gave me a potted history of the entire family and I hung up the phone not only having John's mother's telephone number but also knowing everything about the rose garden the dear man had cultivated and nurtured over many years.

Next came the really hard bit and I decided to leave it until the next day. I had always put my heart and soul into the contacts I made because I knew how important success was to my clients. But I had never wanted a reunion to succeed as much as this one.

The next day Paula and John came into the office and I told them I would ring Jennifer as soon as the ARMS social work student came on duty and I could escape to the back room and make the call without disruption. I asked them to ring me in the afternoon when hopefully I would have something to tell them. They said they would stay in town and pop back later in the day.

Again, with my heart thumping into my throat, I picked up the phone and dialled, preparing myself for the possibility that the woman would hang up or that she might be with people and would not be able to talk. Or perhaps she would be so overwhelmed by my call that she would burst into tears. A woman answered and I began my well-rehearsed spiel.

I asked if her name had been Jennifer ______ and when she said it had I knew that I had John's mother on the telephone. My voice cracked as I told her I was a social worker and that I was ringing on behalf of a young man who was born on such-and-such a date and I wondered if she might know who I was talking about. Jennifer paused for a moment and then slowly answered yes. And then nothing. I continued, telling her that if she had someone with her and could not talk she could say that I was conducting a survey and I would call her back when she was not busy. The phone went quiet and after what seemed like an eternity she replied that she could not talk now but that she would ring me back. I gave Jennifer my number and hung up.

I had done a few initial contacts by now and this one did not have a good feel to it. This woman was hesitant and I didn't think she had written down my telephone number. I had done my best to prepare John for the possibility that his mother might not feel she could go ahead with a reunion. Nevertheless, I dreaded John and Paula coming back to the office. This was not the news I had been hoping to give them.

That night I went to bed feeling anxious and with a pain in my chest. I loved my friends and I wanted Jennifer to get to know them as I did. John was a kind and gentle man with a lovely family and I felt sure that if she just took the chance to meet him she would not regret it. But I had all but forgotten the turmoil she must be going through, having been approached after nearly thirty-five years, and being asked to relive one of the most painful experiences of her life.

I had all but given up hearing from Jennifer when I took a telephone call and heard the distinctive sound of coins being pushed through a slot into a metal box, indicating the person was ringing from a public phone. I crossed my fingers and said the usual, 'Hello, ARMS. May I help you?'

Jennifer had not written down ARMS number because she was so frightened by the call she could not think beyond getting off the phone as quickly as possible. When she finally pulled herself together she rang every number combination she could remember and after many twenty cent coins she got the right place.

My excitement disappeared as she told me the reasons why she could never meet her son. Jennifer already had two young children when she became pregnant and she was told she would lose her daughters if she did not give up the baby. She cried when she told me she was being made to choose between the two children she already had and her unborn baby, and that in the end she could not bear the possibility of losing them all. As she spoke I thought of the 1982 film *Sophie's Choice* and how the young mother had been made to choose between her two children and how her decision haunted her for the rest of her life.

Jennifer said that eventually she remarried but her new husband did not know about the baby and neither did her now grown up family. Her old fears re-emerged and through stifled sobs she told me that she was terrified her husband would leave and that her children would never speak to her again if she told them about her son. I had no idea whether her fears were irrational or entirely realistic.

Mothers did not always like talking with social workers – they associated them with the loss of their babies – and talking about my own experience was sometimes the only way I could bridge the gap between a woman's distrust of me and her taking the chance to stay engaged in conversation a minute or two longer. I could hear how distressed Jennifer was becoming just thinking about having to tell her family and so I told that I understood her feelings because, although I was a social worker, I was also a relinquishing mother.

She seemed to relax a little, and as she talked I began to connect with what she might be going through and I let go of wanting to hear her say she would meet her son.

Jennifer's fear was familiar and I knew that if I were in her situation I would feel it too. Even though my husband and friends had known about me for years and I was relatively 'out in the open', I was still afraid I would be rejected by people when I told them about the adoption for the first time. And as I listened to her I knew that no matter how sad it might be for John and Paula – and me – I must not press her further about a reunion.

As Jennifer was about to hang up I asked if she had ever talked to anyone about her loss. She had not. I told her about ARMS and that it provided support to all mothers who had lost babies through adoption, not just the ones who wanted to meet their children. I said I would be happy to meet her at the office or somewhere else if she just wanted to talk 'mother to mother', and to my astonishment she said she would like that very much. We agreed to meet at the Botanical Gardens in a week's time, and when I tentatively asked if she would like me to bring a picture of John, again she surprised me by saying, 'That would be nice. Thank you.' It was hard to contain my excitement and the glimmer of hope I now felt.

I rang John that evening and told him what had happened, but that he should still not get his hopes up. Meeting Jennifer away from the office meant that she was still extremely nervous and I would not be surprised if she changed her mind about coming at the last moment. I talked to John about the fact that, if she did decide to meet me, I would not push her to have contact with him. No doubt he felt frustrated, but he cared about this woman he had never met, and he did not want to upset her. He agreed that I should be there to support her and if she changed her mind and decided to meet him that would be a bonus. I asked him if he had a photo he would like me to give Jennifer and a few days later I received a lovely picture, which was a very good likeness.

The Botanical Gardens was the perfect venue for a first meeting between a mother and her newly found son or daughter and ARMS used it a lot when the weather was good. The grounds were dotted with exotic trees and shrubs, and rolling lawns fell away to ponds bobbing with lily pads. Black swans and hybrid ducks waddled about the shallows and nuzzled in the mud for juicy tidbits for their babies. This calm place had a way of diffusing the awkward shyness mothers and children sometimes felt when they were meeting for the first time.

The visit with Jennifer came on one of those warm breezy days perfect for an amble in the park. As I walked the half a kilometre from ARMS's office to the Botanical Gardens with John's photo carefully wrapped in tissue paper I hoped the beautiful weather was a good omen. We had agreed to meet at a spot along a curved path near the front of the Gardens, and as I rounded the bend there was no mistaking who was sitting on the wooden seat just ahead of me. John's mother was a very attractive woman and I could see the resemblance between her and her son immediately. She looked up and smiled. There it was – John's smile on this lovely stranger's face. We hugged and I sat down next to her.

A bond exists between mothers who have lost children through adoption and even when words are not expressed they feel they are with someone who implicitly understands them and who will not need to ask, 'Why did you do it?' I felt that warmth with John's mother as soon as we started talking. Her voice was slow and measured like John's, but its lilt was decidedly feminine. I smiled at the similarities in their features and skin colouring and I wanted to tell her just how much like her son she was. But I did not want to overwhelm her. I was afraid she would run away if I did.

After a few minutes I cautiously asked Jennifer if she would like to see a picture of John. She took the photo from me and before I could say anything about him she began talking and I simply could not believe what I was hearing.

'I've told my husband,' she said. 'And I'm sending letters to my girls telling them too. I lost my son once because of what other people wanted, and now he's found me I'm not going to lose him again.'

I was speechless. It was the last thing I had expected to hear from this mother. At best I had thought John might get a note from Jennifer explaining why she could never meet him. The fact that this seemingly timid woman had changed her mind in only a week, and had already told her husband, was nothing short of remarkable. Sometimes it took months for mothers in these circumstances just to return a call, much less accept a photo and then say what Jennifer said next.

'I want to meet him,' she said, staring at the picture and wiping tears from her eyes. I touched her hand and began to explain that I knew a lot about her son and that he was one of my closest friends. Several days later they met for the first time and began to catch up on what had happened in their lives since their separation.

John and Jennifer have now known one another for over twenty years. Christmases and family gatherings are filled with extended family members and the fit is comfortable and relaxed. And among them is an additional and most unexpected relative.

A few years after John and Jennifer were reunited John got a call from a woman saying she was his sister, given up for adoption as a baby. John was surprised because Jennifer had never mentioned another child and he asked the caller how she knew they were related. The woman, who was some years older than John, explained she had received identifying information about her mother from Family Information Service and she had found her through a marriage search. She told John that she understood she had three brothers and that he was one of them.

John told the woman as gently as he could that the Service must have got it wrong because his mother had daughters and he was the only boy. The woman seemed confused and asked if the name she had been given was his mother's name. To John's amazement, it was. But it was not Jennifer. It was his adoptive mother whom he had adored and who died when he was just a teenager.

John hardly knew what to think. His mother had never mentioned a baby and he had always thought that it was she who could not have children. But when he asked his adoptive father if he knew about a child given up for adoption he said it was true. A baby girl had been born before the two had met and when they married they were not able to have children together and so they adopted John and his siblings. John recalled some of his adoptive mother's behaviour when he was young and so much of it began to make sense to him. Her sadness, the lost look on her face sometimes, the private tears she never wanted to explain.

John met his adoptive mother's daughter and although they are not biologically related he said he immediately felt a strong connection with her.

'It was so special meeting Mum's daughter for the first time,' he said. 'She looked just like my mother who died when I was eighteen. It was like I was seeing her again. It was just wonderful.'

Against all my predictions John was reunited with his mother. And not only did it happen, it worked. Jennifer's courage was awe-inspiring, and John's patience and careful consideration of his mother's needs was the special ingredient that has made it last the test of time – which is no small feat among reunions.

After John and Jennifer's reunion I made a resolution. In future I would get someone else to do an initial contact where the client was a personal friend of mine. I had been so over-involved in John's reunion that I could barely sleep at night. It is hard wading into people's lives and trying to convince two strangers that they should meet just because they have a biological connection. And anyone who has dared to walk into the mire of adoption reunion will know just how fraught it is. If it had gone wrong I would have blamed myself, and maybe that would have been the right call. I was pretending I was doing the contact as ARMS social worker, but I was not being remotely professional. If I had been, I would have realised that I should never have taken the case. These were my friends, not my clients.

In the early days at ARMS we learnt as we went along. Every experience was new and many of our strategies had never been tested before. There were no textbooks on how to conduct reunions and ARMS was the first mothers support group to employ social workers to take on that role. I was ARMS first social worker, but I was also a mother who had lost a child through adoption. It was a complicated business all round. But I also know I confused my professional responsibility with my personal relationship and that I should have known better.

23

The Blame Game

IF YOU ASKED MOTHERS who they blamed for having to give their babies up for adoption you might be surprised by the answer. Fathers did not seem to feature very highly on the responsibility register, and although many mothers blamed their parents for not supporting them it was often believed that social workers had betrayed them the most. Mothers had thought social workers would be there to help them, but instead they felt bullied and pressured by the workers until they gave up and gave in.

Mothers said hospital social workers had become angry when they were ambivalent about giving up their babies. They believed the workers colluded with the hospital hierarchy and that by their inaction they sanctioned inhumane treatment of the very people who were supposed to be their clients. Many mothers believed that in reality they were never clients of the social worker, or valued patients of the hospital. They were simply repositories for babies that were to be given to more deserving married couples, and no one was looking after the mothers at all.

Mothers said the social workers who took their consents were just as bad. They did not tell girls that, although they only signed a consent for 'adoption', the truth was that their babies might spend their lives in institutions or foster care without their mother's knowledge. Some mothers said that the workers did not tell them they could revoke consent and others said they did withdraw permission and were told that it was too late when, in fact, there was still time.

The mothers saw the social work profession as ignoring its own code of ethics regarding client self-determination and that pregnant girls and young unmarried mothers were always secondary to the needs of the prospective adoptive parents. And when mothers were told that many of the people they called 'social workers' were probably almoners or administrators they saw it as just another excuse by the profession to try and wheedle its way out of any responsibility for what it had and had not done.

It was against this backdrop of discontent and distrust that ARMS in South Australia made the radical decision to employ a social worker to provide counselling to its mothers. The decision was not immediately appreciated by all ARMS members in South Australia or interstate. Some felt ARMS had sold out by taking government funding in the first place, and others believed that the only people who really knew mothers' issues, and should be counselling them, were other mothers.

Of course, ARMS first social worker was also a mother and so it was a fairly safe introduction to the notion that social workers could be allies rather than enemies. Nevertheless, when ARMS came to employ its next staff member she was chosen entirely on her professional merits and she had no personal experience of adoption at all.

The new social worker said that initially it was difficult following on from a social worker who was also a mother. Sometimes women would ring and when they found out she was a social worker and not a mother too they would sound disappointed or somewhat suspicious of her motives. She thought it must have been much easier for an ARMS social worker who had dual status. Over lunch one day I explained to her that it could also be difficult to have a foot in both camps. Some mothers remained dubious about me because I was a social worker, and some Department staff were wary because I had once been a client, albeit involuntarily, of the system they were now administering. I told the new worker a true story that I hoped would illustrate my point.

Valma had gone to work with Jigsaw and the story had got around that ARMS's new co-ordinator was a qualified social worker.

When I started work I visited all the relevant agencies to introduce myself and to talk about what services I hoped to provide. Most people knew me from my earlier days at ARMS, but one new social worker had not met me before and after being introduced she took me aside and said, 'Oh, I am so glad ARMS has decided to employ a social worker and not another birth mother. I was always concerned about the fact it was being managed by birth mothers and staffed by them as well.' I decided I should break the news to her gently rather than leave it for someone else to explain that she had made a grand faux pas. The poor woman turned scarlet and I felt sorry for her as she stumbled through a lengthy, and rather unnecessary, apology. It was, nonetheless, a lesson learned – for both of us. For her it was probably: 'Never assume anything!' And for me it was recognising that I could have all the qualifications under the sun but if I wanted to work in an agency that handled anything to do with adoption my personal status was always going to be a factor – and not always a positive one.

The new ARMS social worker listened to my story and seemed relieved to know that although there might be pluses to being a mother as well as a social worker at the organisation, there were definitely some minuses as well.

The counsellors who came later probably had it a little easier because ARMS mothers had come to realise that as long as the worker understood their various needs it did not really matter if she had not shared their experience. The management committee could also see the value in having a staff member who had not been on the committee as I had, and who was not confused about her status as an employee. It was something I had struggled with throughout my employment at ARMS and there were ructions from time to time when I wanted to have the decision-making powers I used to have on the management committee but which were not appropriate for an employee. It was not an uncommon issue when a management committee member became a staff member, and ARMS came to believe that life could be much simpler when their employees had no prior personal affiliation with the agency.

Trisha O'Dea came to ARMS in 1993 with a background working in adoptions in Ireland where she was a member of the social work team that assessed prospective adoptive parents and took consents from mothers. Trisha had grown more uneasy about her role in the adoption process and when she moved to Australia she had not thought about returning to that area of social work. However, when she saw the ARMS position she decided that working with mothers was an area that sat more comfortably with her emerging thoughts on adoption and she was delighted when she was offered the job.

Trisha's early observation of the relationship between ARMS and some government departments was that her expertise and the ARMS agency as a whole were generally undervalued. She was surprised at how different it was from her previous job where she was a government employed social worker and her and her agency's legitimacy were not questioned. However, after a change of departmental staff Trisha believed a more cordial and collaborative relationship developed between the two organisations. The Department seemed to be becoming more comfortable referring clients to ARMS, and given that no other State in Australia had entrusted a group for mothers with funding to provide professional counselling services the relationship between the two agencies was working well.

Trisha believed that ARMS, and she as its social worker, might not have been as open as they could have been to the views of mothers who said they voluntarily relinquished their babies because they knew adoption would 'legitimise' their children and their lives would be better with adoptive families. In the early days of ARMS there seemed to be a presumption that all mothers must have been coerced into adoption and that none of them could possibly have done it voluntarily. And I have no doubt that this view slopped over into my own practice when I was ARMS social worker. Despite seeking outside professional supervision to deal with my own potential biases I feel sure I did not validate mothers' experiences quite as quickly when they were different from the generally accepted ARMS position – and where they differed from my own personal account of adoption.

Trisha's thoughts on the early life of ARMS demonstrated an agency in transition from being a self-help group with perhaps a pre-conceived set of ideas, to becoming a valuable, and valued, organisation that was beginning to recognise the diversity of experiences that existed in adoption.

Rose Rawady came to ARMS in 1996 and she picked up on the question of whether or not the social work profession did have a part to play in some of the negative aspects of mothers' experiences. As a social worker herself she knew that one of the profession's basic principles was to strive for social equality and social justice, and that meant advocating for vulnerable and disadvantaged people who often had no voice of their own. Rose knew that many mothers had needed such an advocate while they were in systems that treated them with little or no regard, and that her profession had either not listened to the mothers' calls or it was absent from the process altogether. She felt that even though social workers might have been trying to act ethically and morally they may still have played a part in the significant disempowerment of many mothers. And if mothers were to begin to resolve their grief and anger there needed to be some open and honest dialogue between them and the government agents who had traditionally held much of the power in the decision to relinquish.

Rose Rawady, and nearly every ARMS member around Australia, had heard about the New Zealand-born social worker Murray Ryburn who had travelled from Birmingham in the United Kingdom to be at the 1994 Australian Adoption Conference in Sydney. He had stood up from his seat in the audience and apologised to mothers for the role he, as a social worker, had played in taking their children from them.

> *I listen to the rage and grief and despair of birthparents, and I cannot say that I am okay, that I personally didn't do this or I personally don't do this now. I want to say, now, to the birthparents here that I am desperately saddened by, and sorry for, the things that I as a social worker have done, as a member of that profession,*

to them. I apologise as a social worker for my neglect, my acts of coercion, my failures as someone with a moral, ethical, legal, and paid duty to care, who did not always do so … we must say – I must say – I am responsible. I am sorry.

Murray Ryburn received a loud and affirming applause for his speech. Many delegates at the conference admired his honest and courageous stance and after the event they thanked him personally. Mothers hugged him. They had never believed anyone associated with adoption would ever say they were sorry. Murray Ryburn's apology had meant they could keep fighting for recognition of what had happened to them and their children because at last someone had heard what they were saying and had validated their experience.

Rose Rawady had heard mothers who had been at the 1994 conference talking about what Murray's remarkable apology had meant to them, and how it paralleled the National Senate Enquiry debate and the 'Bringing Them Home' Report on forced removal of Aboriginal children. ARMS was asking what role an apology might play in the larger process of Aboriginal reconciliation and what else needed to happen to make it meaningful. And no one had missed the similarity between what had happened to Aboriginal families and what had been done to young single non-Aboriginal women in Australia, allegedly in the best interest of children.

With the spirit and intent of what Murray had done fixed in her mind, and a belief that her own profession could play a significant role in releasing mothers from some of their torment, Rose Rawady decided to keep the momentum going. She prepared a paper for the 1997 Adoption Conference, which included asking the Australian Association of Social Workers if it might like to extend a formal apology on behalf of its membership. She wrote to the AASW with her idea and received a polite but clear 'No thank you' from the Association. Undeterred, Rose finalised her paper and submitted it to the Conference Committee. It was accepted.

On 12 June 1997, three days before the Brisbane Adoption

Conference, the AASW issued the following statement at its own social workers conference:

> The Australian Association of Social Workers Ltd (AASW) expresses its extreme regret at the lifelong pain experienced by many women who have relinquished their children for adoption.
>
> In doing this we recognise that decisions taken in the past, although based on the best knowledge of the time, and made with the best of intentions, may nevertheless have been fundamentally flawed.
>
> Many individuals and professions, social workers included, were in the past involved in the process that led mothers to give up their children for adoption. With the wisdom of hindsight, and with an awareness of the knowledge, resource, and support now available, we believe that in the same situations today, the same individuals and professionals would give very different advice. This in no way diminishes the pain felt by the mothers and children who were separated at birth.
>
> (AASW Social Work Conference, 12 June 1997)

The AASW 1997 'Expression of Regret' tabled at the social workers conference was not presented at the Australian Adoption Conference and nor was it released to the media for mothers and the general public to read.

Several days later at the conference Rose Rawady delivered her paper and tackled head-on the subject of reconciliation between mothers and the social work profession. She told the story of ARMS SA's unique relationship with social workers and her role working *with* mothers as her clients, and *for* them as her employers. And after surprising her audience with the knowledge that mothers and social workers could and, at ARMS, did co-exist co-operatively she moved to the topic of reconciliation and how it was possible and desirable for the social work profession to make a formal apology to mothers. And there was more. Rose said that it must not simply end with an apology. If it were to have significance the social work profession must have meaningful dialogue with mothers around what had gone wrong in adoption and make sure it did not happen again.

Rose Rawady was not suggesting that social workers were solely responsible for mothers' negative experiences and she recognised that in the past the term 'social worker' had very often been used incorrectly. But she did see that her profession could now facilitate positive change by accepting its share of responsibility and by pushing for a government inquiry into adoption. Rose wanted her profession to show that it was not prepared to give in to more powerful interests where they impacted upon the rights and self-determination of vulnerable people. As well as identifying what the government adoption agencies could have done differently – and must do better in future – Rose saw that the AASW could use the outcomes of the inquiry to put pressure on the larger health, church and welfare systems to look at their own practices, to accept responsibility where warranted, and to improve services for the current and next generations.

Rose Rawady had become her profession's conscience by suggesting it had contributed to a wrong that had been done to many mothers and that it needed to make amends for it. It was a gutsy move by a young social worker who had more to lose than she had to gain by challenging the practices of the agencies that were the largest employers of social workers in Australia. By her actions, Rose Rawady demonstrated everything she believed her profession stood for and, as she had hoped, other social workers began to speak up as well.

In June 1998, prompted by growing agitation from mothers' groups and other interested parties – including social workers – the New South Wales Parliament asked for an inquiry into adoption practices in that State between 1950 and 1998. The following year a Tasmanian Joint Select Committee reported on its adoption services between 1950 and 1988 and the State's *Mercury* newspaper reported that as an outcome of the inquiry a number of politicians had apologised to mothers whose children had been taken through forced adoption. Other States began reviewing their past adoption practices and each waited with interest to see the outcomes of the inquiries already underway.

It was, nonetheless, another ten years before the notion of a federal inquiry was seriously considered and it came when the Western Australia Parliament made an apology to people affected by forced adoption. In the process of making its formal apology Western Australia recommended that a federal inquiry be conducted into the whole matter of adoption in this country. The Senate responded by referring to the Community Affairs Reference Committee an inquiry into former forced adoption policies and practices. Over the next months the Senate Inquiry into Forced Adoption conducted public hearings around Australia and it received over 400 submissions from individuals, groups and agencies. One of them was from Dr Susan Gair.

Dr Gair had been aware the Senate Inquiry into Forced Adoption was underway and that the social work profession was perhaps being judged unfairly based on the practices of others. She was a member of a national committee working towards social work registration with the National Registration and Accreditation Scheme. Lack of registration and accreditation were problems that had dogged the profession for years because without registration social workers could continue to practice without any ongoing professional development. Worse still, people could call themselves social workers without having had a single day's training. And this was exactly the issue that had irritated social workers when mothers were blaming the profession for acting unethically in its adoption practices. Undoubtedly some of those so-called social workers were not social work trained at all but everyone was being tarred with the same brush.

Dr Gair joined with the AASW to make a submission to the Senate Inquiry into Forced Adoption and in it she included a study she had done some years earlier when she interviewed twenty social workers who had worked in adoptions in Queensland between 1960 and 1990. Dr Gair had asked the social workers if they thought the profession owed mothers an apology. Around two thirds of the workers said they were of two minds but they agreed that it should probably occur – but with one major qualification. They would only agree to an apology if it was stated that the people coercing mothers might have called themselves social workers but that they were probably not qualified social workers at all. The social workers in Dr Gair's study did not doubt what mothers had been saying. They just wanted to make sure the full circumstances of who might and who might not actually have been a social worker was understood.

The AASW's submission to the Senate Inquiry acknowledged the past injustices towards parents and children in adoption. It described the reality that some employees, although thought to be social workers, would not have been trained practitioners. And having qualified its position the AASW acknowledged that in any profession, including its own, a minority of workers failed to meet the standards of the profession. Additionally, the past actions of some social workers as agents of government policy had contributed to the pain and loss experienced by all parties to the adoption process. The AASW recognised that instead of challenging systems some social workers had been 'co-opted to uphold and enact unjust practices' and that those actions were 'in contravention of core values of social work such as human dignity and worth, social justice and self-determination …'

It was by no means an easy thing for the AASW to declare. And perhaps believing it may need to redeem itself with the Senate Committee reading its submission – and with its own profession who were not exactly unanimous about acknowledging any fault – the AASW stated that in more recent times the social work profession may well have become part of the remedy. And it was right to mention it. Adoptions social workers had supported the introduction of the Adoption Contact Registers in the late 1970s and they had been strong advocates for records to be opened so that secrecy was no longer a feature of adoption practice in Australia. And in order to ensure that no one can call her or himself a social worker without training, the AASW remains committed to lobbying the Federal Government for social work to become a registered and regulated profession in Australia. The AASW concluded its submission by recommending that the government could extend an apology if the evidence in the Senate Inquiry indicated it was warranted and if it would help the nation's healing.

In the winter of 2012 the AASW published in its *National Bulletin* another acknowledgement to birth mothers forced to relinquish their children. It included the paragraph submitted to the Senate Inquiry acknowledging the role of some social workers and saying that their practices were not in keeping with core social work values and may have also contravened Commonwealth and State policies. The acknowledgement concluded by reiterating that although social work may have been part of the problem in the past, it was now active in advocating for outcomes that were more client-focused.

The *National Bulletin*'s acknowledgement did not receive one positive reply from its readers. It did, however, receive several rebuttals. One incensed social worker reminded the AASW that most so-called social workers were not trained and she doubted if there were more than twenty qualified social workers nationally working with single mothers during the 1950s and 1960s – at a time when some 45,000 adoptions were granted. The retired worker was also outraged that the acknowledgement was alleging, without any evidence, that social workers' practices might have been unethical and illegal. She went on to question the AASW's acceptance of the Senate Inquiry's findings, believing it relied heavily on allegations by mothers who were mostly anonymous, and that the AASW trusting the Senate Report 'without qualification', was in itself 'unprofessional'. The social worker ended her angry response by reiterating the critical need for the profession to gain registration if it were ever to properly protect its clients and itself from those who would call themselves social workers but who had no qualifications.

A second social worker wrote that, other than Dr Gair's study, little research had been done into social workers and their role in adoption practices and it was too soon to make definitive judgements about how effective, or otherwise, the profession might have been. She believed that attributing responsibility to social workers for coercing mothers and not telling them their rights implied an overall deficiency in the profession's practice. She felt that lack of evidence was an issue and that, where it had been proven that social workers had acted unprofessionally they should be dealt with, but where allegations had not been substantiated the AASW must not suggest anything to the contrary and it must stand by its members.

The acknowledgement to mothers was published in the AASW *National Bulletin* where social workers could read it, but it was not published more broadly so people affected by forced adoption could see it. It could also be accessed on the AASW website but after the negative feedback from members the acknowledgement was removed. AASW president Professor Karen Healy responded in the next *National Bulletin* and said that the acknowledgement had been intended to record the profession's sorrow for those subjected to forced adoptions and she was sincerely sorry for any offence it had caused to social workers. Professor Healy ended her apology to the AASW members: 'I hope that as the AASW engages in the difficult task of recording and remembering our past that we do so in ways that do justice to all those concerned.'

Consultation with AASW members had occurred before the acknowledgement was put in the *National Bulletin* and no one registered opposition to the idea. It was not until after it was published that the AASW realised how strongly some social workers felt about the issue, and that making any official apology to mothers was going to require further consideration.

To an outsider it seemed somewhat odd that the social work profession's first attempts at 'acknowledging some regret' were never distributed further than the people who were supposed to be doing the acknowledging. It was rumoured that some individual AASW branches had also attempted acknowledgements over the years but, again, they were never seen by the people to whom they were addressed. And it was sadly ironic that after two very genuine, albeit cautious, attempts by the AASW as a whole to begin the process of making an apology to people affected by forced adoption, the only apology it actually extended was to the social work profession for making the acknowledgement in the first place!

When Rose Rawady stood up at the 1997 Adoption Conference and said that she knew mothers who had lost children through adoption could work side by side with social workers without acrimony, she was talking from experience. Her predecessors at ARMS, and those who would follow her, would all say that it was one of the most professionally rewarding jobs they had ever had. Of course it was hard work, and the hours were generally longer than anyone was paid for, but their clients trusted them, and so did their employers. They were able to show mothers that social workers could be there to support them in their goals and that although the profession might, rightly or wrongly, have been accused of not being there to help them in the past, it was here to help them now.

On the matter of an apology from the social work profession to mothers, no firm decision has yet been made. There is merit in the argument that a profession should not be apologising for the sins of others, and there is evidence that many of the people mothers believed to be social workers were not from that profession at all. Having said that, one cannot help but go back to social worker Murray Ryburn, who stood up at the Adoption Conference in 1994 and apologised unreservedly for the part he believed he played in the sadness and grief experienced by mothers who lost babies through adoption. Through his apology he showed he was prepared to look at his own practice and acknowledge where he believed it was wrong. His were the actions of a social worker demonstrating the values and ethics of his profession and rather than being seen to collude with a corrupt system Murray Ryburn was lauded as a hero by the adoption movement. His actions allowed social workers like Rose Rawady, and those who followed her, to stand up and say they also believed the profession should apologise for the part it wittingly or unwittingly played in what went wrong in adoption. And, more importantly, that their profession would ensure it never happens again.

24

An Amazing Bunch of Women

LIKE EARLIER CONFERENCES, the 1997 Brisbane program included some amazing ARMS women. Trisha O'Dea had taken time off her new job to deliver her paper, 'The Experience of Adoption Reunion for the Relinquishing Mother'. Rose Rawady spoke to her controversial paper 'Partnership or Seeking Common Ground? Social Work and Self-help for Natural Mothers; Towards a Process of Reconciliation'. Long-time ARMS management committee members Maureen Craig, Evelyn Robinson and Pam Longley presented a joint paper: 'What does Reconciliation Mean for Natural Mothers?' And Evelyn Robinson delivered a separate paper 'Grief Associated with the Loss of Children to Adoption'.

Maureen had been an ARMS member since the 1980s and her energy was still high. Over the years she had taken on most of the roles on the management committee and her knowledge was vast. There were few subjects she could not talk about with some authority, and she was an exceptional speaker.

Pam approached ARMS in 1992 around the date of her son's birthday wanting to speak to someone about the question of contact. Pam had married the father, Graham, and in 1990 they received information through the South Australian law changes giving them their son's name. They sat on the information because Pam had been told not to approach her son while still young. Two years had now passed and she wanted to know if ARMS would write to him on her behalf. ARMS agreed, and in the meantime she started attending the support groups.

The group meetings proved to be inspirational to Pam and the mothers in ARMS helped her to start her own journey of discovery. She began by telling her family that she and her husband did have a child, a son, and that he had been adopted as a baby. It was a difficult disclosure but she knew that at last the lie had been exposed and she had reclaimed part of herself. Pam began to understand her own experience and eventually began writing letters to the editor and speaking on talkback radio. It was something that a few years earlier she would never have imagined possible. Graham came to one or two support meetings but, finding them a bit too deep and meaningful, he decided to support his wife in other ways. Pam acknowledged that, if truth be known, she was pleased that ARMS was primarily her domain. Part of her wanted to keep her experience exclusive. After all, it was she who had given birth to their child. In 1993 Pam joined the management committee and Graham helped out by making stands and banners and anything else ARMS needed for its trading tables and education displays.

Pam and Graham's son responded to the first letter ARMS sent. He shared information with them but there was no talk of a meeting. When Trisha O'Dea joined ARMS in mid 1993 she agreed to write to the couple's son again. This time he agreed to meet with his mother.

The meeting between Pam and her son took place at the Hackney office. The chairs were a bit tatty by now but the cottage still had a comfortable warmth that felt right for a reunion. It was a place where Pam had always felt at home and she hoped her husband would understand that she needed to have the first meeting with their son at ARMS, and on her own.

When Trisha brought Pam's son into the room she felt all the things other mothers had described. That incredible sense of wonder. Dreaming of the child and being met by an adult. And still wanting to hold this young man in her arms as though he were a baby. Above all, knowing she had to keep those feelings to herself so not to overwhelm him. Pam and her son talked for several hours and Trisha took photos of the two of them together. Graham did not meet his son and he and Pam remain respectful of the young man's right to maintain his privacy.

ARMS wanted a bold display to accompany the stalls the mothers took on their educational programs around South Australia. The women decided upon a cream calico banner with ARMS name and logo, and a smattering of hearts. In 1993 Pam joined the mothers in setting up a stall in Rymill Park where they tied their new banner to a tree to mark International Women's Day. ARMS mothers had been too nervous to walk in the march but they wanted to be part of the celebration and so they decided to meet the other groups afterwards. By 1994 the courage of their convictions had strengthened and the mothers joined the other women's groups in Victoria Square and together they marched proudly with their banner to celebrate International Women's Day. After the march they erected their display and draped the ARMS banner in front of the trestle covered with brochures, books and other items for sale.

To mark the turn of the new century, ARMS got a small grant to go towards making a new banner. Graham got out his tools and hammered away attaching to wooden poles the three-metre-long bright yellow material with its strong black ARMS name and logo. Some mothers wore complementary yellow T-shirts as they stood behind the vibrant sign. From now on no one seeing the march was going to miss this group of women, or their message.

Mothers in ARMS had come a long way. These women were now writing in journals, speaking at conferences, taking their issues 'on the road', joining marches, publicly debating surrogacy and artificial insemination by donor practices, and protesting about adoption programs taking children from Third World countries to satisfy the diminishing supply of available babies in Australia.

Between 1995 and 2000 Pam spoke at the Multidisciplinary Conference of the Royal College of Nursing, The National Association of Loss and Grief Conference, The National Council for the Single Mother and her Child Conference, and two national adoption conferences. As treasurer she lobbied the government for funds to outreach to Port Pirie, Whyalla, Mount Gambier and the Riverland, and also participated in some of those country programs. Pam had worked with ARMS for over a decade and, like many others who had spent endless hours meeting bureaucratic demands so ARMS could continue supporting mothers, she was exhausted. A family tragedy had also taken its toll and Pam stepped off the management committee so she could lead a quieter life with Graham. She still keeps in touch with a small group of ARMS friends. The bond between mothers is never really broken.

Evelyn had also come to ARMS to seek support from other mothers. She was at university in Scotland when she became pregnant and her son was born in the United Kingdom. Evelyn immigrated to Australia and in the late 1980s decided she wanted to talk to someone about the loss of her son. ARMS had been taking social work students for a number of years and Jennifer Schaffer (who remained ARMS consultant for many years after she graduated) helped Evelyn work through the grief and loss she had hidden away over the years. And when she and her son established contact, and he said he was coming to Australia to meet her, Evelyn asked if ARMS would meet with them together to talk about what they might expect from reunion. It was a role ARMS had played informally when mothers shared experiences at support meetings. However, this was the first time it had formed part of the professional counselling service and included both parties together at the beginning of their reunion. It was a good idea and as more reunions took place ARMS began to provide a greater range of educational options for newly reunited mothers, fathers and children.

Evelyn joined the management committee in 1993 and became so committed to the work ARMS was doing that she decided to change career from teaching to social work. She gained her qualification in 1996. In 1999 Evelyn's application for the position as ARMS counsellor/co-ordinator was successful and she relished her new role. By this time ARMS had moved from the cottage in Hackney to the edge of the Adelaide central business district.

For a long time the government had been talking about collecting a group of non-government organisations in one large building. The attraction for ARMS was that the rent would be government subsidised and the office would be relatively close to the centre of the city. And, no doubt, there would be an inside toilet! In 1997 ARMS got the all-clear to move into its new office in Torrens Building. The 1880 arch-fronted Italian-Renaissance-style building had been built to complement the Supreme Court, Treasury and other government buildings situated in tree-filled Victoria Square. The government had refurbished the building and the wide mahogany staircase that took staff and visitors to its upstairs offices declared an opulence that ARMS had not experienced before.

Torrens Building was as far removed from the little two-roomed cottage at Hackney as one could possibly imagine. Some loved the new space; others thought mothers would worry about the lack of anonymity when they walked into ARMS off the busy square. As it happened, Torrens Building, although not as cosy as the Hackney office, provided a central easy-to-access location, and those walking in off the street could have been going to any of a number of offices housed in the building. In reality, their confidentiality was probably better protected in the city than it had ever been at the Hackney address. But mothers remained divided. Some would continue to say that the tatty rooms of the first ARMS office had a warmth that was never duplicated. Others loved the plush new surroundings and felt this was what the mothers deserved.

ARMS was always in need of money to buy a new piece of equipment, or to help fund the newsletter that was now being sent all over the world. Pauline, ARMS administrator since 1992, helped mothers arrange garage sales, cake stalls, and even a fashion parade to raise money. They never stopped trying to come up with new and innovative ways to promote the service and help with the organisation's running costs.

ARMS also held luncheons twice a year so mothers could get together in a social setting where the focus would be on enjoyment rather than talking about the sad events of the past. The midyear lunch initiated by Evelyn and called 'Not the Christmas Lunch' was particularly popular. A Mother's Day lunch was also held annually so women could drop into the office and be with someone if they were feeling low. For a time the Mother's Day phone-in was reintroduced as well. ARMS knew that many mothers felt overwhelmed on that 'special day' and the lunch and the phone-in gave them somewhere to go, or someone to talk to, if they needed it. And although some of the issues were the same as they had been when the first phone-in was conducted in 1983 there were also stark differences. Some mothers were ringing in because their reunions had stalled, or their children had simply said they did not want to know them. Others did not know the laws had changed and that they might be able to find their children. Many just wanted to talk to another mother. The women rostered on the phones said that the Mother's Day phone-in, although always emotional, meant a lot to them. It was a way they could give others the support that had been given to them when they first contacted ARMS.

In line with the need for outreach services, Evelyn set up an ARMS support group at the Southern Women's Health Service so that people who lived in the ever-expanding southern suburbs could come to a meeting without having to travel into the city. A significant proportion of ARMS service involved conducting reunions and supporting families after contact and Evelyn began exploring the current post-relinquishment grief counselling model that had traditionally been used at ARMS. She could see that grief for mothers who had lost children through adoption was different from other kinds of grief and she developed a therapy that included aspects of re-grief therapy and disenfranchised grief. Evelyn wrote extensively on the topic and shared her knowledge worldwide. In 2000 she wrote a book, *Adoption And Loss: The Hidden Grief*, and the following year she went on her first overseas tour talking about her work at ARMS and the disenfranchised grief experienced by mothers who had lost children to adoption.

There were many issues to tackle at ARMS and Evelyn remembered working with families where rape or incest had resulted in pregnancy. Contrary to popular belief that mothers never wanted to find children conceived under such traumatic circumstances, Evelyn helped more than one mother and her newly found son or daughter explore and resolve issues around the circumstances of the child's birth. Genetic sexual attraction was another phenomenon that had not been known before adoption records were opened. Sometimes mothers asked ARMS to help them deal with the 'funny feelings' they were having for these people whom they had just met. They knew they were their children but they were also adults and strangers. Some adopted adults expressed the same confusion. They talked about feelings of 'being in love' with their parent and thinking there must be something wrong with them because they felt that way. In time it became accepted as a not uncommon feeling during the euphoric first stages of reunion and mothers and their adult children were reassured that, if they did experience such feelings, they generally went away as the relationship became more established. Evelyn made sure she kept on top of any new research because ARMS was at the cutting-edge of what was happening when parents and children met for the first time. She was also sharing the unique knowledge she was gaining in this specialised area by submitting articles to journals, writing pamphlets, and delivering papers in Australia and overseas.

Evelyn worked at ARMS until 2003 and sadly her leaving was traumatic and acrimonious. There were serious differences of opinion between Evelyn and the committee and she believed the issues primarily revolved around work role expectations. Accusations flew back and forth and eventually Evelyn sought external advice on the best way to manage the situation. Unfortunately, nothing seemed to shift the fundamental divide that existed between employer and employee and after months of frustration on both sides Evelyn resigned. Such was her hurt and anger that a year later she resigned her membership and resolved that she would not be involved with the organisation again.

When I approached ARMS for its perspective on the rift that had caused Evelyn to leave, the chairperson felt it would be a breach of confidentiality to comment on such a work matter even though many years had passed. It was evident, nonetheless, that Evelyn's resignation was a huge loss for ARMS and the mothers who had to say goodbye to an exceptional staff member and friend.

Evelyn continued her work to educate the community about issues for mothers. She wrote three more books, *Adoption and Recovery: Solving the Mystery of Reunion*, *Adoption Reunion: Ecstasy or Agony?* and *Adoption Separation: Then and Now*. Today Evelyn is considered an expert on disenfranchised grief in adoption and on adoption reunion. She speaks at conferences and seminars nationally and internationally and still writes prolifically for journals and other publications.

In March 2013, Evelyn joined Australia's ARMS groups and other mothers who had been trailblazers in adoption reform at a dinner in Canberra to celebrate thirty years of mothers' groups fighting for the rights of people affected by forced adoption. It was a special occasion and unfortunately many of the women who had made a real difference over the years could not be there. But it was right that Evelyn should be sitting at one of the tables. Her contribution to ARMS and the adoption movement as a whole was, and remains, remarkable.

Donna had found out about ARMS through Jigsaw. Her son had approached her and she needed to talk to someone about how to go about responding to his contact. ARMS took her through the steps of reunion and talked to her about what, realistically, might happen. Donna was also given literature to read as she had not even begun to deal with the pregnancy when her son made contact. And when Donna went to her first support meeting she said her 'mouth just fell open'. She could not get over the fact that other women had been told the same things as she was told when she had her baby. 'It's over now. That's it. Get on with your life. Forget about it.' And when Donna told her story for the first time she said, 'It was like a weight lifted off my shoulders.'

Donna said she had benefited so much from being with other mothers she felt she wanted to give something back. She did not know much about politics but she could help organise funding events and social occasions, and with this in mind she joined the management committee. Donna had heard about a company that provided buses to take people on shopping trips where the organiser received a percentage of what was spent on the day. A group of mothers signed up for the outing and everyone had a lovely time, including two people who were on the bus and who, until then, had never known anything about adoption or the mothers who had lost their children. Sometimes it was a meal and a movie. And at ARMS twentieth anniversary the chairperson organised a guest speaker and two guitarists to play music at a lavish cocktail party. It was held in the central courtyard of Torrens Building and everyone who attended said it was a grand evening. The courtyard was also used for afternoon teas with the emphasis on relaxing in between the difficult business of dealing with loss and grief, shame and stigma. The mothers set up tables and chairs with colourful cloths and napkins, pretty china cups and saucers and sprays of garden flowers spilling over the rims of simple vases. Everyone brought a plate of food to share, and sometimes champagne, and there was lots of laughter and chatter.

Donna had described herself as a shy person who did not mix well. She had always seen herself as not being good enough because of what had happened to her when she was young. But when she joined a group of women who did not judge her she began to come out of herself. And she found that when she talked about her son's adoption to her family and friends they did not judge her either. 'I received a huge bunch of flowers from my daughter-in-law's mother,' Donna said. 'And when she handed the flowers to me she said, "This is what you didn't get thirty-six years ago."' The gesture by Donna's extended family was an act of validation and kindness she will never forget.

Robyn joined ARMS in 2003. She had read about ARMS in a brochure the Department had given her. She was nervous about going to a meeting because although she did know a number of adopted people she had never met a birth mother. Robyn said that none of the people who were supporting her through her pregnancy told her about the grief she would feel for the rest of her life. Neither she, nor they, had any insight into how it would affect her later on.

Robyn did not have formal counselling with ARMS but she found the support groups invaluable. She wanted to be respectful of her daughter's right to privacy. At the same time she wanted her to know she would be there if ever her daughter wanted to see her. Those situations were always tricky and it was to her credit that she sought the wisdom and support of others.

Going on the management committee was not Robyn's intention. She simply found herself there and so got on with the business of being ARMS secretary. Robyn had come from the private sector and was astounded at how tight money was for ARMS. The photocopier was old and dilapidated but there was no money to buy a new one. And if ARMS needed new equipment, or materials for an outreach program, or money for a banner, it had to apply for grants, and an exceptional amount of time was involved in getting the submissions done. Maureen and Meg, another stand-out committee member, were holding down day jobs as well as doing ARMS work and Robyn was amazed at their commitment and stamina. She did not see how ARMS could keep going with so much to do and so few people on the committee to do it.

In around 2007 Robyn resigned from the management committee after a change in her day job but she kept in touch with the ARMS mothers. Among her fondest memories were the Mother's Day afternoon teas in the Torrens Building courtyard.

Mireille joined ARMS in 1996 after she and her husband were contacted by their son. They were extremely excited about meeting him as it was something they had always hoped would happen. Nevertheless, there were children and other family to tell and Mireille thought she and her husband might benefit from some counselling through ARMS. It was not long before the mothers told her that it seemed Mireille's husband was coping well, but she was not. Mireille was still harbouring strong feelings of anger and hurt and the loss of their son was not something she and her husband had really talked about. With ARMS support, and Evelyn helping her explore her unresolved grief, Mireille was able to meet her son without imposing upon him her own sense of loss.

Mireille and her husband went to a couple of meetings together but like Pam's husband he eventually realised they had different needs and that ARMS was more useful to his wife than it was to him. Mireille could never have imagined that she would 'come out' as publicly as she ultimately did. She joined the ARMS Whyalla outreach team, talking with social workers about adoption and going on television to tell people about her personal experience. It was scary being so exposed but Mireille said she felt empowered, and safe, because she had ARMS mothers by her side.

There were a few years when Mireille spent less time at ARMS. Her husband was seriously ill and in 2006 he died. She was grateful that he had had ten years with the son he had lost through adoption. When she returned to ARMS, Mireille had a renewed enthusiasm about giving something back to the mothers from whom she had gained so much over the years. She continued speaking up about adoption and supporting the mothers who had shared her experience.

And then there were the mothers who came to the support meetings and who believed their contribution was negligible. But they were often the first port of call for new visitors and they shared a warmth and kindness that made people feel they could return.

Every one of these amazing women played a vital role.

25

Stories in Fabric

MOTHERS HAD LONG ADMIRED a large multi-coloured quilt hanging on the walls of both ARMS offices. The women knew it had been made by mothers in the early 1990s and that it depicted their journey from conception to the adoption of their babies and, for some, reunion. The quilt was made primarily from cotton and calico and around the perimeter were small squares stitched with names and symbols.

The quilt had been the brainchild of Lynne, who came to ARMS in the late 1980s because she had lost a child to adoption. Lynne had a background in textile design and the AIDS quilt had stuck in her mind as a way to help people grieve loved ones lost to the horror virus and at the same time to promote the issue of HIV AIDS to a naïve world.

The idea of making an ARMS quilt did not excite everyone at first mention. Some pictured a group of ladies sitting around cutting out material and sewing. To them it was anti-feminist, promoting the female stereotype of women as homemakers. They preferred educating mothers about gender bias and women's oppression. I was one of the sceptics and I could not have been more wrong.

As the idea of the ARMS quilt began to gel mothers formed small working groups in their homes and at the office. They cut circles and squares and long ribbons of material to form the basis of this visual journey. The central circle depicted the mothers' collective womb and branching out from it like a myriad of octopus legs were the strips of calico, some frayed and torn in a violent end, and others snaking the mother's journey to the outer edge of the quilt.

Away from the group each mother found a piece of material that had personal significance, and in her solitude she quietly stitched her baby's original names or some other meaningful symbol across the little square patch. Each quilted memory was then stitched to another and together they formed the border of the artwork, completing the mothers' individual and shared journey.

The finished quilt was a beautiful experiment that not only produced an exceptional wall-hanging, it bonded women together in a moment when they could sew and laugh and cry and tell their stories through pieces of fabric that had meaning for them. Every woman who participated in making the ARMS quilt, including myself, said how peaceful and soothing it was to be sitting and sewing with other mothers who had shared the journey. And when all the pieces were joined together it was as if all the little children whose names were on the patches had clasped hands encircling their mothers. The symbolism of the quilt was profound and so was the privilege of making it.

The quilt formed the centrepiece for an exhibition, 'Out of the Shadows – the Birth Mother's Story', held at Speakers Corner in Old Parliament House in May 1992. The other feature of the exhibition, the documentary *Bitter Surrender*, ran non-stop for the two months the doors were open. There was a board for people to leave a note to say what they thought about the mothers' experiences of adoption. The vast majority of the little slips were positive but there were still a small number of chilling comments criticising women for giving up their babies and saying they had no right to look for them.

The mothers at Torrens Building office loved the symbolism of the quilt as a memorial to their lost children and wondered if they could add their own squares of textile art to the wall-hanging. The management committee decided the first quilt should remain unaltered and so Fay, a keen quilter, suggested making another. The mothers agreed, deciding to make a commemorative quilt to mark twenty years of ARMS in South Australia in 2003.

Under Fay's tutelage a group of mothers came together and

the design of the ARMS twentieth anniversary quilt began to take shape. The women wanted the new quilt to complement the first ARMS quilt, but it was important that it did not sit in its shadow. A unique quilt would reflect the agency's evolution; ARMS name and constitution had changed in the last twenty years.

In 1995 ARMS changed its constitution, adding to its objectives that it would 'seek an end to adoption and support the creation of more appropriate alternative care options'. ARMS's first constitution had been much less definite on the issue and some would say it had lacked courage by not taking a stand. This constitutional change was not suggesting that children should remain in homes where they were unsafe. On the contrary, ARMS had always been clear about acting in the best interest of children. It was saying that the hallmark of adoption was around falsifying birth certificates, changing children's names and hiding their heritage, and that as adoption was the practice of perpetuating lies it was not something that ARMS could ever support.

In late 1999 ARMS took the next step and removed 'relinquishing' from its name. ARMS had long believed that 'relinquishing' implied that mothers had voluntarily given up their babies, not reflecting the reality for many. ARMS wanted to keep the acronym by which it had been known for sixteen years, and so it decided upon the same name as Western Australia's ARMS group: the Association Representing Mothers Separated from their Children by Adoption. It was a mouthful, and no one used it when they were answering the ARMS phone, but it more accurately described the group the agency served and mothers preferred the new, albeit longwinded, name.

Fay and the group described making the quilt as an experience that brought them closer together. They chatted as they sewed, stopping to listen when mothers talked about the flowers or animals chosen in their pieces of patchwork. Donna told how she wanted to make a fabric jigsaw puzzle with her son's name stitched into one of the pieces. It would stand out from the others and dotted in the background would be little blue hearts. It was her hope that one day that special piece of the jigsaw would find its place and in the meantime she lived in hope. Sometimes there were tears over cups of tea, at other times smiles and praise for a story beautifully stitched. All in all it was the same bonding experience the mothers before them had gone through and the quilted result was just as exquisite.

Each unique piece made by the fifteen mothers who contributed to the twentieth anniversary quilt was filled with metaphor and emotion. In the bottom left-hand corner was a stitched inscription, Natural Mothers Supporting Each Other 1983–2003, and in the centre of the quilt was ARMS now not-so-new name and logo.

In 2004, ARMS psychologist Ann Griffith suggested a written record of the quilt should be produced. An illustrated colour booklet, *Our Quilt Our Memories*, was professionally printed and sold to members to raise funds and as educational gifts to politicians when ARMS met with them. In the front of the booklet Meg, now chairperson, wrote:

> By coming together to share ideas, talent, material scraps and chatter, the Quilt Workshops did what ARMS does best – support natural mothers who have been separated from their children by adoption. This book illustrates each square and contains the mothers' thoughts. For some this was a painful experience, for others a therapeutic one, but for all it embodied the sharing and support which defines ARMS.

Fay and Maureen took the two quilts to a Quilters Guild Exhibition and spoke about what the wall-hangings represented. Initially there was a deathly silence. It was hard to gauge what the reaction meant but the quilts did not get the same warm reception that some of the other exhibits received. Nevertheless, Fay said that standing up in front of people she did not know and talking about women who lost children to adoption was, for her, a proud moment. She was coming out of her shell and telling the world her story, and there would be no turning back.

Lynne and Fay revisited their quilts during the writing of *Mothers in ARMS*. The two women had been at ARMS at different times and had not met before. And neither had seen their special pieces of fabric for many years. The quilts now had a new home at the South Australian History Trust and it was an emotional moment when the two large boxes were opened and the cream dust covers folded back. The quilts looked like sleeping children tucked up safely in cots with soft blankets wrapped around them to keep them warm.

Each quilt was carefully taken out and spread to its full size. The women gently stroked their creations and talked quietly about the various pieces of patchwork and who had sewn them. Memories came flooding back and, amid clicking cameras, one or two tears were wiped away. Lynne wrapped the larger quilt around her body and, as Fay laughed, twirled about the mezzanine like a whirling dervish.

As the calico was drawn up and the quilts were safely tucked away in their boxes, the mothers wondered if this was a fitting resting place for these stories in fabric. Fay and Lynne left the building knowing the quilts were protected, but also feeling a sadness. They were determined that one day the quilts would be seen again in all their finery.

26

A Farewell to ARMS

MEG JOINED ARMS at the beginning of 1998 and by the end of the year she was on the management committee. Like those before her, she wanted to ensure that the ARMS message reached as many people as possible and that the service kept going. She was impressed by the outreach programs rolled out around country South Australia and by the women who took the show on the road. And she smiled at the ingenuity of this group of women who made the most of ARMS central location by putting a sign out on Victoria Square and inviting people in to an open day at the office. It would not be long before Meg was making her own mark on the organisation.

Maureen and Meg made sure that ARMS was always on the political agenda and at least once or twice a year they visited politicians from all parties. The management committee knew ARMS could easily be forgotten and its funding withdrawn if the government was not aware of its vital work. Contact with politicians ensured that the inherent problems within adoption were never forgotten either.

ARMS also had another function. It was the watchdog on all things adoption. And of particular concern was the increase in the number of overseas adoptions following the dramatic decline in babies available locally. Adoptions Australia revealed that 585 adoptions were granted nationally in 2004–2005, an increase of seventeen per cent on the year before. Of that number, seventy-four per cent were overseas adoptions, fifteen per cent were 'known child' adoptions and eleven per cent local adoptions. By the mid 2000s the myth about adoption being in the best interest of children had been well and truly debunked, and helping babies remain within their biological families was now a priority in this country. ARMS wondered how Australia could justify taking babies from mothers in developing countries when it no longer believed it should be taking babies from mothers at home. ARMS also feared that mothers overseas might be losing their children for similar reasons to their sisters in Australia – that they were not abandoning their babies, and that they and their children would spend a lifetime grieving the loss of their family and culture.

ARMS had heard there was to be a Federal Senate Inquiry on Overseas Adoption and the management committee was keen to make a submission on this vital topic. When the Senate Inquiry came to South Australia, Mireille went to the open session in the morning and bravely spoke about ARMS's perspective to a room full of people who she believed did not share her view and who were in favour of overseas adoption. Ann Griffith, Meg, Maureen and Pam appeared before the Inquiry in the afternoon and raised the reasonable question: why would any government want to inflict the same kind of suffering on women and children from other countries? It was a harrowing experience and Meg said she left the meeting feeling that ARMS's position had not been respected and that the Inquiry members were pre-disposed to quite a different position.

The Inquiry findings were released in November 2005 and among the recommendations was a request that the Federal Government take a much stronger role in managing overseas adoptions, including negotiating new adoption programs with more countries. Needless to say the findings were not received warmly by ARMS, nor by those government agencies concerned about the practice of overseas adoption. Although the Inquiry findings were considered, ultimately a decision was made to minimise the number of overseas adoptions to Australia. Children from past inter-country programs like Korea, India and Vietnam were adults now and they were saying loud and clear that inter-country adoption did not always work. Like the Aboriginal children taken from their families and 'assimilated' in non-Aboriginal homes, inter-country adoptees did not always feel they were accepted into white Anglo-Saxon Australia, no matter how well-loved they were by their adoptive families. Some felt a yearning to go home to their countries of birth to find out who they were. And when they did, some of them found that they were not orphans at all and nor had they been abandoned by their families.

Although many of the overseas adoption programs were discontinued, division remained on the issue of whether children from other countries needed homes and, if they did, whether more funding should be provided to help them stay in their own countries rather than take them away from their families, culture and heritage.

In March 2008, the Australian Broadcasting Corporation's *7.30 Report* presented key arguments for and against, and Meg was invited to participate on behalf of ARMS. Deborra-Lee Furness, a well-known proponent of overseas adoption and wife of film star Hugh Jackman, was also interviewed, as were prospective adopters and an adult adoptee born in Vietnam in 1973.

The program commenced with the prospective adopters talking about how difficult it had become to adopt a child and that the people on waiting lists were into their thousands while the numbers of available children were now only in their hundreds. Deborra-Lee Furness responded passionately. 'People want these children. You've got them wanting them and you've got the orphans desperately needing love and food and nourishment and what's stopping them is the bureaucracy in the middle, and I see this as a priority. We're saving lives.' It was an argument that resonated with a lot of people at first thought and, like Ms Furness, they could not understand why Australia could not just pick up these infants and bring them home.

Bronwyn Bishop who chaired the Parliamentary Overseas Adoption Inquiry to which ARMS had made its submission several years earlier, appeared to support Ms Furness's argument by saying the Inquiry found that there was an 'anti-adoption culture that permeates the entire bureaucracy'. Ms Bishop did not say why such a view might have been prevalent within government departments but left the impression that she believed it inappropriate that bureaucrats should feel negatively towards adoption.

Meg responded. 'I think it's a great injustice to do that to communities in developing countries where we don't have that practice here in Australia any more. It's not acceptable and yet we're quite happy to look overseas and take children from developing countries.' And there it was – ARMS argument in a nutshell. If Australia no longer believed in adoption – and Ms Bishop was indeed right that governments had come to see adoption as not necessarily being in the best interest of children or their parents – how could this country believe it was all right to adopt babies and children from countries outside Australia?

Lynelle Beveridge from the Inter-Country Adoptee Support Network said: 'We need to address the broader context of an inter-country adoption and especially the post-adoption side of that for the adult adoptees once they grow older as well as for their families because there are issues once the child arrives. It's not just that's the end of the story. That's only just the beginning of the journey.'

Deborra-Lee Furness had the last word on the current affairs show, describing some of the horrible things she believed would happen to children if they were left to walk the streets and fend for themselves in their own countries.

It was an emotive argument and it was important that ARMS was there to challenge what would have otherwise looked like an open and shut case in favour of increasing the number of overseas adoptions. Providing a counter-argument to policies designed for the procurement of children for infertile couples was what ARMS had always done extremely well. It had a unique knowledge and perspective on the consequences of separating mothers from their children through adoption, and because of its expertise ARMS was often called on to join the debate on other issues such as surrogacy, donor sperm programs and, of course, overseas adoption. ARMS was also the only agency whose primary focus was the mother, and its purpose was to ensure her rights and needs were always known and represented.

When the South Australian Government advertised it was going to fund a post-adoption agency ARMS hastily put in a submission. Relationships Australia won the tender and in mid 2006 it opened the Post Adoption Support Services (PASS) in Adelaide. It was a generic service for adopted people, mothers, fathers, adoptive families, siblings, and anyone else who might have an issue around local or overseas adoption. It was a comprehensive, well-funded service and it could more than adequately attend to the counselling and support needs of ARMS mothers. However, by its very nature, PASS needed to remain impartial and equally committed to all people affected by adoption. Only ARMS could take up the political activist role on matters that affected mothers whose needs might be at odds with other parties in adoption. If ARMS were to close up shop one of the key functions of the organisation would be lost forever.

Meg and Maureen were acutely aware that the hours they were devoting to ARMS were getting longer and the numbers of people offering to help them were decreasing. Sometimes they did not have a quorum at management committee meetings and decisions had to be put off until they could find enough people. Member numbers were also dwindling and each annual general meeting had less participants than the year before. There were fewer mothers wanting counselling as well, but the bureaucratic requirements of keeping the agency going seemed to be on the rise.

The other worrying factor was that the opening of the Post Adoption Support Services meant there was the real possibility that ARMS could lose its funding. Perhaps the government would feel it was doing enough by funding just one adoption counselling service. It was demanding work managing all the vagaries associated with running ARMS and the women were near exhaustion. The writing was on the wall.

Gillian, ARMS founding chairperson, had returned to the group in around 2005 after meeting her daughter. By 2007 she was ensconced on the management committee again and it was not long before it was obvious to her that ARMS was floundering.

Mireille was also aware that ARMS's days were numbered. She wanted to make sure that a new home was found for the mothers before ARMS's doors closed forever and she and Gillian started talking to Nikki Hartmann, head of the Post Adoption Support Services, about the possibility of PASS finding a place for the ARMS mothers within its service. Naturally, PASS was agreeable to the idea but it did not try to push ARMS into making any quick decisions. It knew that ARMS had to work through this crisis on its own and that PASS would be there if and when it was needed.

ARMS was determined to hang on just a little longer. It decided to lobby members one more time, hoping enough people would nominate for the management committee to keep the agency's head above water. Curiously, it was able to get people who were prepared to help ARMS wind down, but it could not find enough members who were committed to keeping it going. Meg, Maureen and Gillian met with PASS several times to look at the transition from one agency to another and it became clear that 2009 would be ARMS last year. A small group was established to close the service, led by Gillian who had been ARMS first chairperson.

Naturally members had mixed feelings about the end of ARMS. Some were terribly upset and felt they had lost their home. Others were just sad that everyone was so tired they could not hang on any longer. But as Gillian said, there were also positive reflections on how far mothers had come.

'We had many conversations,' she said. 'Feeling sad that it was closing down ... but then feeling happy that women didn't need to be silent any more. They didn't need to do public awareness any more or walk down the street with a banner. There was no more having to do things behind closed doors.' And of course she was right. She was one of the mothers who had been at the very first meeting in 1983 when Harri said, 'Welcome, mothers. Yes, you are mothers.' When Gillian looked back down the road she could see that mothers in ARMS had, indeed, come a very long way.

For Meg and Maureen it was a mixture of sadness and immense relief. Maureen was ARMS longest serving management committee member; she had been through the ups and downs of the group for over twenty-two years. Meg had also devoted more hours to ARMS service than she cared to remember, and between them and the other mothers who had served ARMS it was time to hang up the shingle and move on. The women packed up twenty-six years of records and artefacts, and after keeping the boxes in Maureen's home for far longer than she had planned they were sent to the State Library to be stored safely in its secure archives. The quilts were gently folded and taken to the South Australian History Trust to be kept in a temperature and dust-controlled building along with many of the State's other fragile treasures.

Before it finally closed its doors ARMS had one last function. The mothers aptly called it A Farewell To ARMS. Everyone who had belonged to ARMS was invited to celebrate its twenty-six years of service and although many could not be located, and others had died, there was still a good turnout of mothers from across the decades. And as they sipped bubbly and drank tea they laughed and reminisced about 'the good old days'. It was strange to think that such a terrible experience had brought them together and yet here they were looking back with warm affection about their time at ARMS. And there was not one of them who did not leave ARMS the better for having been part of it.

At the end of the evening they hugged and cried and waved goodbye. What they did not know was that some of them would carry the ARMS name one more time. And they would be part of something that all those years earlier no mother would have ever dreamed possible.

27

Believed at Last

ARMS MAY HAVE CLOSED but some mothers were still catching up with one another as friends or at the midyear and Xmas lunches, and the Post Adoption Support Services was running a monthly group for those who wanted the structure of a regular get together.

Some mothers had joined an on-line mailing list set up a couple of years earlier by New South Wales mother and PhD student Christine Cole. In the 1990s Christine had belonged to Mothers for Contact with a woman called Dian Wellfare and ARMS NSW founder Judy McHutchison. In 1993 Judy and Dian became the first mothers to try and sue the government in the Supreme Court, arguing the adoption of their children was illegal. It was anticipated that Dian's case would go first. However, after a five-year battle Dian Wellfare's case was dropped because it lay outside the statute of limitations. Judy's case was never pursued. During this time Christine established Origins, an organisation that became a formidable force in adoption, but eventually left the group because of a difference of opinion. When she began researching her PhD Christine contacted many adoption-related agencies and kept in touch with them.

In 2008, Prime Minister Kevin Rudd made the Apology to the Stolen Generation, a formal apology to the Aboriginal community for Australia's past actions of forcibly taking Aboriginal children from their families and placing them with non-Aboriginal adoptive parents or in foster homes, allegedly in the best interest of the child. It had taken many years for Australia to finally say, 'We are sorry.'

After the Apology Chris contacted people who had been asking her when the government was going to apologise to the non-Aboriginal women who had also had their babies stolen. Chris had long been a political activist in the area of adoption and she decided to set up an on-line network called the Apology Alliance, its primary purpose being to lobby for an apology to that other group of women who had their children taken from them allegedly in the best interest of the child. At the Ninth National Adoption Conference in 2008 when Chris launched her book *Releasing the Past: Mothers' Stories of their Stolen Babies* she also took the opportunity to announce the official commencement of the campaign to achieve both State and federal apologies. The Apology Alliance had galvanised into a credible national lobby group and it was also working hard to counteract Deborra-Lee Furness's zealous attempts to increase the numbers of overseas adoptions into this country.

Through Christine Cole and the Apology Alliance's efforts over a number of years the States began to recognise that families affected by past adoption practices might genuinely be deserving of an unqualified apology. Western Australia was the first cab off the rank, and as part of its apology it recommended that the Commonwealth Government conduct a Senate Inquiry into past adoption practices in this country. The findings were damning. Among the recommendations were that States and Territories, and the Commonwealth Government, 'should each issue a formal statement of apology that identifies the actions and policies that resulted in forced adoptions and acknowledges, on behalf of the nation, the harm suffered by many parents whose children were forcibly removed and by the children who were separated from their parents'.

On 18 July 2012, people affected by forced adoption practices in South Australia, including ARMS and PASS mothers, met at Parliament House to hear Premier Jay Weatherill deliver his apology on behalf of the South Australian Parliament. The Premier said, 'We accept with profound sorrow that many mothers did not give informed consent to the adoption of their children.' And, 'To those mothers who were denied the opportunity to love and care for their children, we are deeply sorry.' He went on, 'To those people adopted as children who were denied the opportunity to be loved and cared for by their families of origin, we are deeply sorry.' The apology concluded: 'To those people who were disbelieved for so long, we hear you now, we acknowledge your pain, and we offer you our unreserved and sincere regret and sorrow for those injustices.'

People clutched hands with strangers sitting next to them and listened in amazement as the government acknowledged that what mothers had been thinking for decades was true. The Leader of the Opposition called past adoption practices 'unethical, immoral and in many instances illegal'. Ms Redmond went on to say that 'as a mother of three children, I find the brutality and sheer inhumanity of all that has happened quite difficult to accept'. And so it went on.

At the conclusion of the apology mothers, fathers, children, families and other guests stood and clapped. But there were no smiles. This was simply a 'thank you, at last you believe us' acknowledgement from the people who, in the past, had been told their stories were make-believe and that no civilised society would ever treat a person so badly simply because she was not married.

As people left the grey marbled building they were met by a throng of journalists jostling for a good spot where they could grab a mother, preferably with her recently found child, to find out what they made of the Premier's apology. The ARMS mothers met at the foot of the slate steps and embraced one another. Some had tear-stained cheeks, others looked overwhelmed with emotion, many looked drained. It had been a long thirty years for the mothers in ARMS.

At the more private affair across the road from Parliament House, the Premier thanked Evelyn, Maureen and Meg for the tireless hours they had put into helping him and his team develop the apology to South Australia. When Evelyn walked back from receiving her flowers I grabbed her arm. We had not seen one another in nearly twenty years. We exchanged numbers and agreed to catch up soon.

And as I waved goodbye to Maureen and Meg I turned and said, 'You know, someone should write the history of ARMS in South Australia. What an amazing bunch of women.'

In early 2013, mothers, children and families from all around Australia received invitations to the country's capital, Canberra, on 21 March 2013 to witness the Prime Minister of Australia, Julia Gillard, make a National Apology to People Affected by Past Forced Adoption Policies and Practices (the National Apology).

28

A National Apology

THE FOYER OF CANBERRA'S PARLIAMENT HOUSE echoed with the buzz of conversation from a thousand pairs of excited and anxious lips. It was a formidable room, quite unlike the old Parliament House with its regal carpeting and rich mahogany wood panelling. This was a grand spectacle of a building, cold, illustrious; when you passed between its tall columns you knew you were somewhere of consequence, that weighty matters were decided here.

Above the main foyer stretched a long mezzanine, and hidden by a walled area were two secluded spots where visitors could take tea and sit quietly for a few moments. Around the walls stood long scrolls showing key passages from every State government's adoption apology, each chosen for its poignancy. Even though the words were no longer new to the people for whom they were intended they could still make one gasp.

Mothers waved to friends from the various ARMS groups and when they hugged their touch was longer than usual. They were thanking each other silently for the years everyone had put into supporting the cause, and one another; thirty years of tireless work culminating in what they were about to witness. The mothers talked about the people they would have loved to see there but who were unable to make the trip. And of course some of them had died far too early.

Fifteen minutes before the doors to the Great Hall opened the people upstairs joined the visitors in the foyer and a natural line began to snake its way across the marble floor. Strangers introduced themselves and shared stories about why they had travelled to Canberra for the big event. Various support groups, isolated from one another by geography or philosophy, shook hands and held one another in a moment of solidarity. Today each and every one of them could stand tall in the knowledge that their group, or they as individuals, had played a part in bringing about the social and political change that led to this historical event.

Each of the 800 chairs in the Great Hall had a sheet of paper, a small packet of tissues and a flower on it. The paper outlined the morning's events and the flower was to place at the foot of the stage in remembrance of all the people affected by forced adoption. The reason for the tissues was obvious.

Cameras whirred and bright lights shone across the crowd as women, men, young adults and children settled into their seats. Some people looked a little dazed. Others gazed around the Great Hall in awe of the number of people who had found their way to Australia's capital to hear this momentous speech. Someone handed out pink, blue and white bows. The pink and blue were to depict whether the lost child was a girl or a boy. White was for the mother who was never allowed to know the gender of her baby. From another mezzanine at the back of the hall the Woden Valley Girls Choir began to sing and the chatter in the room quietened to a soft murmur.

After the Speaker of the House, Anna Burke, explained the format for the morning an Aboriginal woman blessed the land and an elder stamped a traditional dance, clapping puffs of white dust across the stage as he chanted an indigenous song. And then the Prime Minister, Julia Gillard, stepped onto the stage. The Great Hall was silent, keeping its collective fingers crossed that this would be one of her memorable speeches.

Julia Gillard had a reputation for being a great negotiator and administrator, but she was not always liked when she spoke in public. Sometimes she could sound disingenuous and condescending. At other times she could be absolutely brilliant, such as when she made her famous misogyny speech. 'If he wants to know what misogyny looks like in modern Australia,' she said, referring to the Leader of the Opposition, Tony Abbott, 'he doesn't need a motion in the House of Representatives, he needs a mirror.' The fifteen-minute speech went viral on the internet and Australia's first female Prime Minister's stand on sexism and misogyny was applauded by feminists around the world.

It had been a rocky three years in office for Julia Gillard. The Labor Government had commenced its term with a different Prime Minister, Kevin Rudd, and it was he who had acknowledged what had been done to Aboriginal people in his Apology to the Stolen Generation some years earlier. Although he was well liked by the public he was disliked by a large enough number of his party to warrant his deposition. With little warning he was sacked and Deputy Leader Julia Gillard was installed as the new Prime Minister. Kevin Rudd's ousting was extremely contentious and Julia Gillard only just scraped in at the next election. Rumours about her not being up to the job dogged her throughout her elected term, some claiming the Rudd camp from within the party was white-anting her to make her so unpopular that the former Prime Minister would be returned to what he saw as his rightful position. The first challenge to her position was unsuccessful. There were rumours another spill was about to be called and everyone at the National Apology just hoped it would not be today.

The Prime Minister began by saying:

> Today, this Parliament, on behalf of the Australian people, takes responsibility and apologises for the policies and practices that forced the separation of mothers from their babies, which created a lifelong legacy of pain and suffering.

Julia Gillard spoke with passion and poignancy and there was not one person in the Great Hall who did not believe that every word was genuine. She went on:

> We deplore the shameful practices that denied you, the mothers, your fundamental rights and responsibilities to love and care for your children. You were not legally or socially acknowledged as their mothers. And you were yourselves deprived of care and support.

People began to sob.

> To you, the mothers who were betrayed by a system that gave you no choice and subjected you to manipulation, mistreatment and malpractice, we apologise.
>
> We say sorry to you, the mothers who were denied knowledge of your rights, which meant you could not provide informed consent. You were given false assurances. You were forced to endure the coercion and brutality of practices that were unethical, dishonest and in many cases illegal.
>
> We know you have suffered enduring effects from these practices forced upon you by others. For the loss, the grief, the disempowerment, the stigmatisation and the guilt, we say sorry.

If anyone had doubted whether she would get it right, they were worried no more. She had captured in those few sentences everything mothers needed to hear. She understood their experience, she validated their pain and she said the practice was illegal.

Julia Gillard went on to acknowledge the children.

> To each of you who were adopted or removed, who were led to believe your mother had rejected you and who were denied the opportunity to grow up with your family and community of origin and to connect with your culture, we say sorry.
>
> We apologise to the sons and daughters who grew up not knowing how much you were wanted and loved.
>
> We acknowledge that many of you still experience a constant struggle with identity, uncertainty and loss, and feel a persistent tension between loyalty to one family and yearning for another.

Again, she captured perfectly what adopted people had been feeling for generations and from the floor of the Great Hall you could see middle-aged ladies clutching the hands of grown-up sons and daughters as they bent over and wept openly.

And there was another group the Prime Minister acknowledged.

> To you, the fathers, who were excluded from the lives of your children and deprived of the dignity of recognition on your children's birth records, we say sorry. We acknowledge your loss and grief.

Julia Gillard had not forgotten the men who had been denied their rights by a system that discouraged mothers from naming them in a formal way.

The Prime Minister then acknowledged the people who had unwittingly become embroiled in the anguish and disturbance that adoption produced by virtue of being a family member.

> We recognise that the consequences of forced adoption practices continue to resonate through many, many lives. To you, the siblings, grandparents, partners and other family members who have shared in the pain and suffering of your loved ones or who were unable to share their lives, we say sorry.

And finally the Prime Minister said:

> To those who have fought for the truth to be heard, we hear you now. We acknowledge that many of you have suffered in silence for far too long.

The mothers in ARMS turned to one another and nodded. They knew they were included in that acknowledgement. They had fought for thirty years for the myth about adoption to be exposed and they had finally been heard.

It was a remarkable speech and as the Prime Minister walked back to her seat the entire room rose and clapped. It was not to say, 'Well done. You sounded great.' It was to tell her that she had got it right. She had reflected exactly what people felt and she had shown genuine sorrow and regret for what had happened to the tens of thousands of people affected by forced adoption. Her words were not jangly platitudes. They were powerful statements that seeped through small cracks in the brick walls that had held mothers upright for years. The women slumped back in their chairs overwhelmed by the speech they had just heard.

The Leader of the Opposition's speech was less spectacular. Unlike the Prime Minister he had not sought the advice of a reference group to help him word his apology – and it showed. He commenced by acknowledging the eloquent words of the Prime Minister and then went on to talk about a good friend who had had a baby in difficult circumstances.

He said, 'Instead of love there was reproach. Instead of support, rejection. Instead of celebration, silence. And instead of justice, there was wrongdoing.' They were fine words.

And then it went terribly wrong. Tony Abbott looked down into the audience and said, 'We honour the birth parents, including fathers, who have always loved their children.' The front of the Hall erupted and groans could be heard from others in the grand room. The Leader of the Opposition had not done his homework. Mothers had long since rejected any word preceding 'mother' and they were not about to put up with someone supposedly making a genuine apology using such out-dated and inappropriate language. 'We are not "birth" mothers. We are mothers!' they called out. Abbott apologised, and went on.

'We honour those adoptive parents who have tried to do the right thing by their children,' he said.

By this time even the most polite mother in the Great Hall was shaking her head. People were yelling from the floor and all the man could do was try and apologise by saying he would retract what he had said. The problem was that he did not know what it was that had caused so much anger. He did not understand that young girls had been told they were undeserving of being mothers and that only married people could be considered worthy of having babies – their babies. They had lived in the murky shadows with a stain on them while the adoptive parents had raised their children as if they were their own. Mothers saw adoptive parents as having got everything. They did not hate them. But they did not want to have to 'honour them', especially not on the day their own pain and suffering was being acknowledged. It would have been as if Kevin Rudd had asked the Aboriginal people at the Stolen Generation Apology to honour all the white Australians who took their children in. It was the wrong time and the wrong place.

The final straw for many came when the Leader of the Opposition said, 'Whenever adoptions take place, they have to be chosen and they have to be for the right reasons.' Again he seemed to miss the point of why everyone was in the Great Hall, and that many mothers could not conceive of any circumstance where adoption would ever be done 'for the right reasons'. Of course, not everyone was totally against adoption, but the man had made so many gaffes by this time he was not likely to be forgiven for the one that, to some, was the least offensive. Tony Abbott concluded his speech amid yells and boos and slunk back to his chair perplexed at what he had said wrong.

Mia Dyson sang the song 'Jesse' but unfortunately everyone was standing and talking loudly by this time, stunned that the first part of the apology could have been so wonderful and the last part so embarrassing. The Speaker returned to the stage to wind up the proceedings but still no one was listening. It seemed as if everyone had lost their sense of protocol and that they just wanted to tell the person next to them what they had thought about the morning.

The choir started singing again and people filed to the front of the Hall to place their flowers on the stage. It was supposed to be a silent moment to remember a child or a mother, or to think about friends long gone. Instead, people milled around shaking their heads in disbelief that two speeches could have been so far apart in their content and appropriateness to the occasion.

Gradually the guests moved out to the foyer where a couple of journalists were filming people's responses to the Apology. However, the media was oddly absent, quite unlike the State apologies where people could not move for reporters and cameramen. People stood around for a while and were greeted by a few politicians and dignitaries who had also attended the Apology. Eventually the guests made their way down to the lawns where lunch was being served under large white marquees and to the music of the daughter of iconic Australian singer/songwriter Slim Dusty.

The lawns were packed with people eating when the news began to filter down that something of a crisis was happening in Parliament House. Evelyn and her son Stephen had gone in to see the National Apology moved in Parliament and both of them felt somewhat underwhelmed by what they heard. They did not know what everyone else in the House knew.

Behind closed doors – that were about to be flung wide open – some Labor politicians were expressing their unease about Julia Gillard's capacity to lead the party to victory at the election set for later in the year. A Labor Party member, Simon Crean, had just announced to the media that he thought the issue should be brought to a head and he was calling for the Labor Caucus to vote on whether Julia Gillard, or someone else, should be Australia's Prime Minister. And he had someone in mind – Kevin Rudd.

The media attention was frenetic and the journalists and cameramen who were supposed to be reporting on the National Apology were, instead, tripping over themselves to see who might be going in or out of Kevin Rudd's office. The Apology had been totally overshadowed by the news that Gillard might be rolled and that Rudd might be coming back. Program hosts apologised profusely to people who had been contacted for post-apology interviews; there was a far greater imperative now and the public needed to be satisfied. The Apology was old news and Julia Gillard announcing that a vote on the leadership would take place at 5.30 pm was now the hot topic.

The marquees emptied. Paper plates and plastic cutlery were dropped into environmentally friendly bins and guests wandered off to catch taxis to the airport or pick up their cars for the long drive home. The National Apology got barely a mention on the evening news, other than to say that it was a shame that such an historic event had been overshadowed by Labor's infighting. As it happened Rudd did not have the numbers to make a viable challenge and he said as much. The man who called the spill was sacked from the front bench of Parliament and numerous other Rudd followers were relegated to the backbench for the duration.

During the following days numerous tweets, Facebook pages and the odd newspaper item said how shocking it was that the government had selfishly aired its dirty laundry on the very day it was supposed to be apologising for what governments had done to mothers and children in adoption. However, apart from a lot of tut-tutting, very few programs went on to talk about the Apology and what it had actually meant. One Sunday morning political affairs program guest talked about the disgusting display by the government and how it usurped a day of national importance. The man then went on to say he thought people at the Apology had overreacted to Tony Abbott's speech and that, overall, the Opposition Leader had done a pretty good job. Of course the program guest had never taken the time to ask mothers why they had reacted to the Abbott speech. He had not understood why they were upset, assuming they were nitpicking.

The National Apology never did get the recognition it deserved, nor did Julia Gillard get the accolades she should have received for delivering such a fine speech to a very critical audience. But to the mothers in ARMS, and the people who attended the National Apology to People Affected by Past Forced Adoption Policies and Practices, nothing could take away the potency of the speech made by Julia Gillard on 21 March 2013. After years of fighting to expose the myth about adoption, mothers had finally been heard and believed, and it would be hard to imagine that anyone could have delivered the Apology better than Australia's first female Prime Minister.

Three months after the National Apology, almost to the day, another challenge was made on the leadership. This time Kevin

Rudd did have the numbers and Julia Gillard resigned from her position as Prime Minister and from politics altogether. At the next election Labor lost power and Tony Abbott became Australia's new Coalition Prime Minister.

29

A Celebration of Thirty Years

THE EMAIL WAS SENT to mothers around Australia. It was an invitation from mothers Jennie Burrows and Judy MacPherson to a dinner at the Canberra Yacht Club on the evening of the National Apology to celebrate the adoption movement's fight for law reform. Some were ARMS mothers and some were mothers who had come together because they had been advocates and activists in their own right for decades. The final chapter in the mothers' movement did not belong to one group alone.

The room was filled to capacity; some mothers sat outside in the main part of the Yacht Club hoping a space would be found for them during the evening. Jennie welcomed everyone and explained that she and Judy had wanted to have the dinner to bring together the women who had fought for over thirty years for the rights of mothers and their children.

Marie Meggitt spoke about the beginning of ARMS in Victoria and how they had fought so hard for mothers, only to be sold out at the last minute in favour of a lobby group who had more clout. But they had soldiered on and at the Victorian adoption apology in 2012 the government had said it would pass legislation to give mothers the right to apply for identifying information – at long last.

Judy McHutchison talked about the early days of ARMS in New South Wales and the phone calls she made to ARMS in Victoria and South Australia for support. It was a reciprocal arrangement and everyone nodded, showing they had valued her support as well. Everyone was learning on the run. They were heady days.

Judy MacPherson, ARMS mother in the Australian Capital Territory for about as long as anyone could remember, talked about how important the groups had been to her. It was a sentiment shared by the Western Australian ARMS group and Lynne, Carmel and Helen nodded in acknowledgement; they had also valued their mentor Shirley and the ARMS sisterhood nationally.

Christine Cole talked about her time with Origins and how she came to start the Apology Alliance. She talked about discoveries she made while doing her PhD and how interesting it was to hear the first group of ARMS mothers tell how ARMS started in Australia.

And I talked about what I had learned about ARMS in South Australia from writing its story and how I believed each State should document its own history so that what happened would never be forgotten. I looked across the room at my friends, and my sister Deirdre who had held my hand during the National Apology, and I said how incredibly proud I was to have been a mother in ARMS.

At the tables people reflected on the mothers who had not lived to see this incredible day. So many funerals, and not all of them due to natural causes. How pleased they would have been to know that at last mothers did get the apology they deserved. The women wondered if it would have made a difference, or if it was the never-ending grief from losing their babies that finally drove their sisters over the edge.

Over coffee the mothers talked about how incredible it was that ARMS had been born at all given how afraid people were when they first joined. How women sat in silence, surprised the stories being told were so similar to their own, and wondering how others could talk so openly about their experiences without falling apart. And how, gradually, each mother gained strength and, in turn, paid it forward by supporting the next mother who walked timidly through the front door.

Truly courageous people are those who do the things they are the most afraid of, and these incredible women from all of the mothers groups had spoken out in spite of their fear of exposure and retaliation. They changed society's perception of adoption and made governments listen to what had really happened when their children were taken from them. And perhaps most important of all they found a way to tell their children they loved them and that they had never been abandoned by their mothers.

The South Australian ARMS mothers talked about how sad it was that their group no longer existed. But they understood why it had happened. ARMS had shone very brightly in South Australia, thanks to a succession of governments who had chosen to keep it funded, and the women and families who had dedicated themselves to making it work. But everyone was exhausted. They wanted to have a life that was not just built around being a mother who had lost a child through adoption. They did not want to hear more stories of loss and anguish, console another mother who had found her child had died before she found him, or have the continual worry about whether or not there was enough money in the coffers to pay the staff. Like all non-government organisations run on a self-help model, ARMS had lived off the smell of an oily rag and the generosity of members who were often holding down day jobs as well as trying to manage a vital support service. And nearly all the people running the show had experienced the same issues as the people they were trying to support; they were helping others while still coming to terms with their own demons. It was a difficult mix and sometimes there were clashes of personality or ideology. That ARMS SA survived for twenty-six years under those conditions was nothing short of remarkable.

Talk turned to the Post Adoption Support Services and everyone agreed it was a fine agency and it had everything the mothers needed. Well except one thing. PASS could not be an advocate for mothers if it conflicted with the needs and rights of its other clients. PASS was a service for all people affected by adoption, not just mothers, and while it could, and had been, an exceptional advocate on adoption matters it could not take sides at the expense of one of the client groups it represented.

Who would be the political activist to fight for mothers in

South Australia in future? Were there any battles yet to be won? Who would keep an eye on South Australia's overseas adoptions programs? And who would keep in touch with the mothers interstate and overseas to fight for their rights and make sure adoption did not revert to how it had been in the past?

The mothers realised that ARMS in South Australia might not have an office or funding now but the other groups had never had much money and they were still hanging in there. ARMS did not have to end simply because it no longer had money to employ staff. The service had existed before the government financed it and there would always be a group of women who would call themselves mothers in ARMS. They would continue to speak at conferences, write books and make films, lobby governments and speak publicly where they thought mothers and children were at risk. They would find a place where the ARMS quilts could be shown to remind people of the past and they would continue to share strategies with people in other countries so they could challenge their own laws and practices. Mothers in ARMS were now part of a national and international network and their office had become a global one.

The celebration dinner ended and everyone said their goodbyes. Some realised they would probably not see one another again. Others hugged, knowing they would stay in touch for the rest of their lives. It had been a long journey and while they were proud of their achievements they knew it would be unwise to rest on their laurels. History has a not so funny way of repeating itself, they thought.

Epilogue

Consent Matters

WHILE I WAS WRITING *Mothers in ARMS* I revisited many long-forgotten issues, and one that kept waking me in the dead of night concerned the adoption consent form.

I discovered the 'anomaly' in South Australia's consent form while I was writing my thesis in 1987 and I was horrified to learn that the *Adoption of Children Act 1967* allowed for babies to be permanently placed in institutions or anywhere else if adoption was not possible. But the consent only authorised adoption and there was nothing on the form to suggest that anything other than adoption could occur without the mother's knowledge and permission.

When I finished writing this book I decided to do some more research. I wondered just how many babies were never adopted and I was curious to know if I was the only mother who had no idea that, despite what I had been told, I had signed my child away to a life that might never include adoption. I also wanted to know if this was an Australia-wide issue and whether witnesses to consents in other States were as ignorant about the true meaning of giving consent to adoption as were the social workers I had interviewed twenty-five years earlier in South Australia.

On the matter of how many babies were never adopted I located a paper delivered at the 1978 Australian Conference on Adoption on behalf of W.C. Langshaw, Director, Department of Youth and Community NSW, which stated that in the past up to twenty per cent of prospective adoptions were deferred for twelve months or more. After paediatric medical checks were introduced in the late

1960s the number of deferred adoptions dropped to around twelve-and-a-half per cent. Most of those babies were eventually adopted, but not all. I looked through ten years of South Australia's community welfare reports but there was no reference to the actual number of babies never adopted. On the information I was able to glean, however, it appeared that between five and ten per cent of all children placed for adoption spent their lives in foster care, institutions or children's homes. And whilst I did find statistics on the number of mothers who consented to their children becoming State Wards this figure fell well short of the number where adoption did not proceed. I could only assume that the remaining placements were made without the mother's written consent and probably without her knowledge.

Next I asked mothers who had lost babies in all Australian States if they had ever been told a consent to adoption actually authorised other forms of permanent care. The answer was a unanimous 'no'. I reviewed forty years of radio, television and print media interviews with mothers, social workers and departmental heads, along with anything else I could get my hands on associated with adoption consent, and nowhere was it ever mentioned that a consent to adoption authorised anything other than adoption. I also looked at consent forms from all States to see if they described the full meaning of giving a consent to 'adoption' and Tasmania's form from around the 1980s was the only one that mentioned anything other than adoption in the fine print. The rest of the States only authorised 'the adoption of the said child'.

Lastly I contacted social workers who witnessed adoption consents to see what they told mothers when they signed the forms. None mentioned to the mothers the additional powers of the consent form and only one worker said she knew they even existed. Retired social worker Margaret McDonald said she didn't tell mothers their babies might not be adopted because it might worry them unnecessarily. She did not seem to recognise that some of her clients had not wanted to give up their babies in the first place and would have refused to give consent if they had known the truth about what they were signing. Certainly the common bullying tactic of telling girls they were selfish if they did not agree to adoption would have failed if mothers had known adoption was not guaranteed and that what they were really consenting to included the possibility of a worse life for their children than they themselves could have offered.

I was astounded at my findings and more than a little surprised that the issue had not been raised before. For a time it was so unbelievable it made me doubt what I was seeing. I began to think about all the mothers who were forced into consenting to adoption and where it never took place, and how angry they and their children who remained in care had a right to be. And I thought about the tens of thousands of mothers like myself who did not give an informed consent because we signed the form under duress and were never told the true meaning of consenting to 'adoption'. I wondered if any consent could be considered valid under those circumstances and I thought I would like to challenge the legality of my consent to adoption even though it was now forty-six years after the event.

As I filed away my research on adoption and wrote the last words for *Mothers in ARMS* I looked back at my experience and thought about what I knew in 1968 and what I know now. And I am left with this gnawing belief that if I or my mother (who had always pressed adoption as the best thing for her grandchild) had ever been told there was the remotest possibility my baby might spend her life in an institution or in a foster home, I would have bundled her up in my arms and with my mother's blessing we would have brought her home.

Acknowledgements

Many mothers agreed to be interviewed for the book but I do not think any of us realised what it was going to be like to resurrect the past and tell it as a piece of social and political history. Of course tears were shed during the interviews – we had all expected that. But it was the growing realisation that the women of ARMS had achieved something remarkable that took us by surprise, and left us with a sense of pride that would have been barely imaginable when the group first formed in 1983.

These are some of the amazing mothers, fathers, children, friends and groups who must be acknowledged for their contribution to ARMS and the story of forced adoption not only in South Australia but Australia-wide. Out of respect for those who wanted to remain relatively anonymous I have only used first names: Barbara, Beth, Brenda, Carmel, Chris, Corinne, Cynthia, Deirdre, Donna, Dorothy, Evelyn, Fay, Gillian, Graham, Helen, Ineka, Jennie, Jennifer, Jo C, Jo F, John, Josie, Joylene, Judith, Judy, Karly, Kay, Lila, Lily, Lorraine, Loryn, Lynne, Marg, Margaret, Maria, Marie, Mary, Maureen, Meg, Mireille, Pam, Pamela, Paula, Pauline, Rhonda, Robyn, Shirley, Sue, Valma, Veronica; ARMS Vic, WA, NSW and ACT, Jigsaw, NCSMC, Origins, Parents for Contact, Parents of Adoptees, Post Adoption Support Services, The Apology Alliance, WIS, and all the mothers in *Bitter Surrender.*

And then there are Harrison Anderson and Ann Sharley, who founded ARMS SA, and Rosemary West (formerly Kiely) who gave ARMS its name. And Francesca da Rimini who made the documentary *Bitter Surrender* with Ann and who loaned it to me so I could describe this groundbreaking film and the courageous women in it.

Others who also kindly gave of their time and shared their unique knowledge and recollections include Cynthia Beare, Peter Bicknell, Dr Christine Cole, Dr John Cornwall, Lex de Man, Dr Susan Gair, Ann Griffith, Nikki Hartmann, Professor Karen Healy,

Susan Lenehan, Margaret McDonald, Dr Sarah Moore, Trisha O'Dea, Professor Marian Quartly, Rose Rawady, Liz Ryburn (wife of the late Murray Ryburn), Professor Dorothy Scott, Sue Vardon and Dana Wortley.

Siblings

Brothers and sisters of children with disability

Kate Strohm

Siblings tells what it is like to grow up with a brother or sister with a disability or illness. The siblings of children with a disability are often the overlooked ones in families struggling to cope.

Kate Strohm, a sibling herself, bravely shares the story of her journey from isolation and confusion to greater understanding and acceptance. She provides a forum for other siblings to describe their challenges and provides them with strategies to make sense of their experiences.

Through the workshops she has presented around Australia and overseas, Kate has been able to incorporate the experience and wisdom of many families and professionals, and provide clear tools for parents and practitioners to support brothers and sisters of those with a disability.

ISBN 978 1 74305 233 4

For more information visit www.wakefieldpress.com.au

Memoirs of a Suburban Girl

A novel

Deb Kandelaars

It is 1979 and a teenage girl is charmed by a man she meets in a disco. Before long, like Alice through the looking glass, she tumbles into a world of strange and frightening characters. Desperate to escape, she takes us into the darkness and out again, delivering her tale with wit, warmth and furious zest.

Memoirs of a Suburban Girl is the cautionary tale of an everyday girl who makes a wrong turn.

ISBN 978 1 86254 955 5

For more information visit www.wakefieldpress.com.au

Clay Gully

Stories from an apple orchard

Sally van Gent

Sally van Gent wonders how to utilise the beautiful land of Clay Gully. Goats? A vineyard? Remembering the sweet fruit she ate as a child she decides to establish a heritage apple orchard. She sets to work – and soon enough, rains falter, bugs, birds and feral animals attack the trees, and a snake takes refuge in the leg of her jeans. As the drought takes its toll and animals in the surrounding bush begin to suffer, Sally fights to keep her orchard alive.

ISBN 978 1 74305 188 7

For more information visit www.wakefieldpress.com.au

Wakefield Press is an independent publishing and distribution company based in Adelaide, South Australia. We love good stories and publish beautiful books. To see our full range of books, please visit our website at www.wakefieldpress.com.au where all titles are available for purchase.

Find us!

Twitter: www.twitter.com/wakefieldpress
Facebook: www.facebook.com/wakefield.press
Instagram: instagram.com/wakefieldpress